INTRODUCTION TO RUBRICS

INTRODUCTION TO RUBRICS

An Assessment Tool to Save Grading Time, Convey Effective Feedback, and Promote Student Learning

Dannelle D. Stevens

Antonia J. Levi

Foreword by Barbara E. Walvoord

SECOND EDITION

STERLING, VIRGINIA

COPYRIGHT © 2013 BY
STYLUS PUBLISHING, LLC.

Published by Stylus Publishing, LLC
22883 Quicksilver Drive
Sterling, Virginia 20166-2102

Stevens, Dannelle D.
    Introduction to rubrics : an assessment tool to save grading time, convey effective feedback, and promote student learning / Dannelle D. Stevens, Antonia Levi ; foreword by Maryellen Weimer.—2nd ed.
        p. cm.
    Includes bibliographical references and index.
ISBN 978-1-57922-587-2 (cloth : alk. paper)
ISBN 978-1-57922-588-9 (pbk. : alk. paper)
ISBN 978-1-57922-589-6 (library networkable e-edition)
ISBN 978-1-57922-590-2 (consumer e-edition)
    1. Grading and marking (Students)
2. Students—Rating of.   I. Levi, Antonia, 1947–   II. Title.
LB3063.S74   2013
371.27′2—dc23

                                    2012010840

13-digit ISBN: 978-1-57922-587-2 (cloth)
13-digit ISBN: 978-1-57922-588-9 (paper)
13-digit ISBN: 978-1-57922-589-6 (library networkable e-edition)
13-digit ISBN: 978-1-57922-590-2 (consumer e-edition)

Printed in the United States of America

All first editions printed on acid free paper that meets the American National Standards Institute Z39-48 Standard.

Bulk Purchases

Quantity discounts are available for use in workshops and for staff development.
Call 1-800-232-0223

First Edition, 2013

10 9 8 7 6 5 4 3 2

To our students

CONTENTS

LIST OF FIGURES

A rubric, the authors emphasize, is a tool. And their book itself is a wonderful tool for exploring how to use rubrics as tools. For a long time, I have been recommending the first edition of *Introduction to Rubrics* to faculty in workshops I lead. I can recommend this second edition with even greater enthusiasm, because it does so much more, and does it so intelligently.

A couple of decades ago, when I first began to use, write about, and recommend rubrics, I didn't even call them by that term. Few faculty members in workshops were familiar with the term, and most did not use formal rubrics, though a few faculty would share with me rubric-like instruments they had developed for themselves and their students. Now, at every campus or conference where I lead workshops on assessment, teaching and learning, or writing across the curriculum, virtually everyone knows what a rubric is. Or thinks they know what a rubric is. Or knows that they hate rubrics, as they hate "assessment." Or finds that rubrics are one of the best learning tools they ever used. Students come into college already familiar with rubrics from high school, bringing their own experiences and emotions about rubrics. For both students and faculty, rubrics have gathered a weight of emotion, especially because of their association with "assessment" requirements. Stevens and Levi simply cut through all of that by explaining that rubrics are tools. The authors illustrate how that tool can be used, and they offer sane, practical advice about all those uses. This book can address a great deal of the puzzlement, misperception, and hostility that sometimes surround rubrics.

Is a rubric worth the time and effort? The authors address that question front and center, helping faculty to make wise decisions about whether to use rubrics and how to make them most effective. Stevens and Levi demonstrate what rubrics are good for, how to construct them, and how to use them in various settings. With a clear and friendly tone, the authors speak teacher-to-teacher. The book is replete with explicit, helpful examples. Phrases such as "we found that" and "we are often surprised by" reflect the authors' own experiences with rubrics and the experiences of colleagues. Short examples and case studies illustrate the many ways in which rubrics can be used.

Research findings help to clarify why and how rubrics can enhance student learning. For example, the authors review research about the kinds of feedback that are most helpful to students and show how rubrics, when used, can provide that feedback.

I regularly use and recommend rubrics for all kinds of situations, but I had never sat down to make a list of all the benefits of rubrics or their many uses. Stevens and Levi include a rich and provocative list, together with detailed and clear explanations of each item on the list.

The authors offer advice about all the surrounding situations and problems that may accompany rubrics: how to get students involved in rubrics, how to use rubrics with T.A.s, how to collaborate with other faculty in constructing common rubrics, and how to use rubrics that someone else has constructed. The book focuses on rubrics but offers a great deal of advice about good teaching, good collaboration, and good assessment. In short, this book is a great tool.

Barbara E. Walvoord

PREFACE TO THE SECOND EDITION

The first edition of *Introduction to Rubrics* was the result of a conversation about the use of rubrics in the classroom. Its focus was on rubric creation and usage in classroom teaching. Since then, we (Dannelle D. Stevens and Antonia Levi) have enjoyed our experiences leading workshops and offering presentations at a wide variety of colleges, universities, and conferences, mostly in North America, the Near East, and Asia. As a result of these experiences, we have become more aware of the numerous ways in which rubrics are used in higher education, including their usage in "hands-on" and community-based learning, scholarly teaching projects, online teaching, career development, and program assessment.

This second edition retains the original six chapters and includes six new chapters, an epilogue, and appendices that build on the methodologies and instructional theories that formed the focus of the first edition to show how they can be adapted to new uses.

Chapter 7, "Making It Yours," discusses whether or not it is useful to adapt existing rubrics (including those found online) rather than creating your own from scratch, and offers suggestions as to how to make adaptations if a ready-made rubric is used.

Chapter 8, "Rubrics for Learning From Experience," addresses how rubrics can add clarity and organization to hands-on learning such as studio and lab work, or field work such as community outreach programs or internships that involve activities outside the classroom and the direct oversight of the professor.

Chapter 9, "Rubrics and Online Learning," builds on Chapter Eight to discuss how rubrics can be used in the virtual classroom when all face-to-face interaction may be gone. It also offers some insights into other adaptations that work well online.

Chapter 10, "Rubrics and Teaching Improvement," offers a case study showing how a professor disaggregated the overall rubric score into the scores on each of the dimensions to assess and improve his own teaching and the learning outcomes for his students. It also offers a more general teaching model showing how rubrics fit into classroom teaching overall.

Chapter 11, "Rubrics for Self-Assessment and Career Advancement," offers insights into how newly minted PhDs seeking a first job or faculty members facing promotion and tenure decisions can use rubrics and university guidelines to document the way in which their work meets or exceeds expectations.

Chapter 12, "Rubrics and Program Assessment," looks at how departments, programs, and entire campuses can use rubrics to assess and document student learning outcomes so that the results are useful and conducive to further improvement. Included are Walvoord's four-hour "no-frills" departmental assessment model, Portland State University's University Studies assessment rubrics, and the VALUE rubrics created by the Association of American Colleges and Universities.

And last but not least, in the epilogue our "Rubrics Manifesto" sets out the reasons why we think rubrics are an essential foundation for the future of higher education and our progress as a diverse and progressive society.

Further Acknowledgments

There is always a place for acknowledgments because this book would not be the book it is without the advice, feedback, and support from others. For reviewing chapters and offering invaluable insights, we thank Candyce Reynolds, Ellen West, Yves Labissiere, Rowanna Carpenter (all from Portland State); Dan Bernstein (University of Kansas); Matt Kaplan; and Deb Meizlish (University of Michigan). Natasha Haugnes offered inspiration on the use of rubrics in art at the Academy of Art University, San Francisco. We applaud Terrel L. Rhodes, Association of American Colleges and Universities, for not only encouraging us but leading the effort to develop the VALUE rubrics for outcomes for a liberal education. Praise and thanks to Barbara Walvoord who has not only contributed the foreword but has written about assessment in a way that makes sense to faculty; and Bob Smallwood, Assistant to the Provost for Assessment, University of Alabama, for acknowledging our work early on and inviting us to work with his faculty.

Besides these specific acknowledgments, we have learned from faculty about how rubrics work in different settings at national and international institutions. The United States higher education institutions are: University of Maryland, University College; University of Detroit, Mercy; University of Hawaii; Alan Hancock Community College, California; Oregon Health Sciences University, School of Nursing; Central Oregon Community College; Oregon Technical Institute; Portland State University; Cal Poly, Pomona; Texas A&M, College Park; and George Washington University, Washington, DC. In addition, there are a number of international universities where we have shared our expertise while gleaning new insights from these settings: Atilim University, Ankara, Turkey; Bethlehem University, Bethlehem, Palestine; Ehime University, Matsuyama City, Japan; Teikyo University, Tokyo.

Finally, to John von Knorring, president and publisher at Stylus Publishing, who believed in us and has helped us craft our work so others can benefit, a hearty and heartfelt thank you.

PREFACE TO THE FIRST EDITION

This book developed out of a conversation about college teaching held in a Turkish coffee shop between a professor of modern Japanese history and popular culture, Dr. Antonia Levi, and a professor of graduate teacher education and educational psychology, Dr. Dannelle Stevens. Dr. Levi was teaching in the interdisciplinary, yearlong freshman core (Freshman Inquiry) and working at adapting her teaching style from mostly lecturing to a more learner-centered, interactive approach. Dr. Stevens was in the midst of a 2-year guest appointment at Bilkent University in Ankara where she was engaged in teaching and running workshops on learner-centered theories and techniques to a new generation of Turkish teachers for whom such ideas were even more radical than they were for a set-in-her-lecturing-ways professor of modern Japanese history. As we talked about the ways in which our academic lives, seemingly so different, overlapped, one word emerged with great regularity: rubric.

Rubrics, we agreed, were one of the handiest aids to educators since the invention of the blackboard. They saved us hours of time when used for grading while providing timely, meaningful feedback to our students. Moreover, when used properly, they became a normal part of classroom teaching, often promoting some of our best class discussion experiences and increasing the rate at which our students became self-motivated, independent learners. We concluded that the only reason more of our colleagues did not use rubrics was that they did not fully understand what they were or how they can improve the teaching experience for any educator.

And so we decided to write a book.

Our Book

Our book is a primer for professors who are considering using rubrics as grading and instructional tools for the first time or who wish to refine their use of rubrics. In this book, we define what rubrics are, explain their basic components, and show a variety of ways in which those components can be arranged and rearranged to suit a variety of needs and disciplines. We include a large number of sample rubrics, but we also describe how professors can construct their own rubrics from scratch using a step-by-step approach, and we show how others, including students, can be involved in rubric construction. We show how we use rubrics to grade student work and to evaluate our own teaching effectiveness. We also discuss the theoretical bases for using rubrics and their importance in conveying meaningful feedback to students in ways that are most likely to result in enhanced learning.

Our Audience

We intend this book to serve primarily as a resource for educators in higher education, including graduate education. We recognize that it may also be useful to teachers in high school, especially those teaching Advanced Placement classes, but on the whole, teachers of K–12 already use rubrics that are better adapted to their needs. These rubrics are designed to reflect the more complex demands professors place on students in higher education.

Acknowledgments

We are grateful to the many friends and colleagues who freely offered their advice and assistance to us as we wrote. To list all who assisted is impossible. This style of rubric creation is above all interactive, and literally hundreds of friends, colleagues, students, and a few total strangers added their input along the way.

We are particularly grateful to Cheryl Ramette, Susan Agre-Kippenham, Suzanna Johnson, Cate Pfeifer, Feride Guven, Serap Emil, and Zeynep Girgin, who shared their time and experience with rubrics in the classroom with us. We are also grateful to the entire PSU Metamorphosis team, including Grace Dillon, Phil Jenks, Teresa Taylor, Ann Marie Trimble, Victoria Parker, Ellen Broido, Dave and Judy Arter, and Kate Gray, who participated in the team-teaching rubric experiment. We would also like to thank Margaret Sands and Arman Ersev of the Graduate School of Education at Bilkent University; Devorah Liebermann, Martha Balshem, and the Center for Academic

Excellence at Portland State University; and Chuck White, Terry Rhodes, Judy Patton, Denise Schmidt, and the many other members of the University Studies Program at Portland State University who contributed their expertise on assessment, e-portfolios, and other innovative rubric uses. Thanks are also due to the members of the Seamless Learning and Transfer Consortium, including members from the National Center for Higher Education, the League for Innovation in the Community College, Portland State University, Alverno College, Georgia State University, Clackamas Community College, Waukesha County Technical College, Georgia Perimeter College, the University System of Maryland, Fund for the Improvement of Post-Secondary Education (which funded our meetings to discuss rubrics and e-portfolios), and especially to Chuck White, who wrote the grants and did a major part of the organizing.

The majority of the rubrics reproduced in this book were developed by the University Studies Program at Portland State and we thank the program; its director, Judy Patton; and participating faculty for permission to use them.

Special thanks are also due to Molly Stevens, who retrieved lost files, straightened out our graphics, and otherwise operated as our chief troubleshooter in cyberspace. And, of course, none of this would have been possible without the invaluable advice and assistance of our editor, John von Knorring of Stylus Publishing.

PART I

AN INTRODUCTION TO RUBRICS

WHAT IS A RUBRIC?

\Ru"bric\, n. [OE. rubriche, OF. rubriche, F. rubrique (cf. it. rubrica), fr. L. rubrica red earth for coloring, red chalk, the title of a law (because written in red), fr. ruber red. See red.] That part of any work in the early manuscripts and typography which was colored red, to distinguish it from other portions. Hence, specifically: (a) A titlepage, or part of it, especially that giving the date and place of printing; also, the initial letters, etc., when printed in red. (b) (Law books) The title of a statute;—so called as being anciently written in red letters.—Bell. (c) (Liturgies) The directions and rules for the conduct of service, formerly written or printed in red; hence, also, an ecclesiastical or episcopal injunction;—usually in the plural.
—*Webster's Unabridged Dictionary*, 1913

Rubric: n. 1: an authoritative rule 2: an explanation or definition of an obscure word in a text [syn: gloss] 3: a heading that is printed in red or in a special type v : adorn with ruby red color.
—WordNet, 1997

Today, a rubric retains its connection to authoritative rule and particularly to "redness." In fact, professors like us who use rubrics often consider them the most effective grading devices since the invention of red ink.

At its most basic, a rubric is a scoring tool that lays out the specific expectations for an assignment. Rubrics divide an assignment into its component parts and provide a detailed description of what constitutes acceptable or unacceptable levels of performance for each of those parts. Rubrics can be used for grading a large variety of assignments and tasks: research papers, book critiques, discussion participation, laboratory reports, portfolios, group work, oral presentations, and more.

Dr. Dannelle Stevens and Dr. Antonia Levi teach at Portland State University in the Graduate School of Education and the University

Studies Program, respectively. Rubrics are used quite extensively for grading at Portland State University, especially in the core University Studies program. One reason for this is that the University Studies Program uses rubrics annually to assess its experimental, interdisciplinary, yearlong Freshman Inquiry core. Because that assessment is carried out by, among others, the faculty who teach Freshman Inquiry, and because most faculty from all departments eventually do teach Freshman Inquiry, this means that the faculty at Portland State are given a chance to see close up what rubrics can do in terms of assessment. Many quickly see the benefits of using rubrics for their own forms of classroom assessment, including grading.

In this book, we will show you what a rubric is, why so many professors at Portland State University are so enthusiastic about rubrics, and how you can construct and use your own rubrics. Based on our own experiences and those of our colleagues, we will also show you how to share the construction or expand the use of rubrics to become an effective part of the teaching process. We will describe the various models of rubric construction and show how different professors have used rubrics in different ways in different classroom contexts and disciplines. All the rubrics used in this book derive from actual use in real classrooms.

Do You Need a Rubric?

How do you know if you need a rubric? One sure sign is if you check off more than three items from the following list:

❑ You are getting carpal tunnel syndrome from writing the same comments on almost every student paper.

❑ It's 3 A.M. The stack of papers on your desk is fast approaching the ceiling. You're already 4 weeks behind in your grading, and it's clear that you won't be finishing it tonight either.

❑ Students often complain that they cannot read the notes you labored so long to produce.

❑ You have graded all your papers and worry that the last ones were graded slightly differently from the first ones.

❑ You want students to complete a complex assignment that integrates all the work over the term and are not sure how to communicate all the varied expectations easily and clearly.

❑ You want students to develop the ability to reflect on ill-structured problems but you aren't sure how to clearly communicate that to them.

❑ You give a carefully planned assignment that you never used before and to your surprise, it takes the whole class period to explain it to students.

❑ You give a long narrative description of the assignment in the syllabus, but the students continually ask two to three questions per class about your expectations.

❑ You are spending long periods of time on the phone with the Writing Center or other tutorial services because the students you sent there are unable to explain the assignments or expectations clearly.

❑ You work with your colleagues and collaborate on designing the same assignments for program courses, yet you wonder if your grading scales are different.

❑ You've sometimes been disappointed by whole assignments because all or most of your class turned out to be unaware of academic expectations so basic that you neglected to mention them (e.g., the need for citations or page numbers).

❑ You have worked very hard to explain the complex end-of-term paper, yet students are starting to regard you as an enemy out to trick them with incomprehensible assignments.

❑ You're starting to wonder if they're right.

Rubrics set you on the path to addressing these concerns.

What Are the Parts of a Rubric?

Rubrics are composed of four basic parts in which the professor sets out the parameters of the assignment. The parties and processes involved in making a rubric can and should vary tremendously, but the basic format remains the same. In its simplest form, the rubric

Title

Task Description

	Scale level 1	Scale level 2	Scale level 3
Dimension 1			
Dimension 2			
Dimension 3			
Dimension 4			

Figure 1.1   Basic rubric grid format.

includes a task description (the assignment), a scale of some sort (levels of achievement, possibly in the form of grades), the dimensions of the assignment (a breakdown of the skills/knowledge involved in the assignment), and descriptions of what constitutes each level of performance (specific feedback) all set out on a grid, as shown in Figure 1.1.

We usually use a simple Microsoft Word table to create our grids using the "elegant" format found in the "auto format" section. Our sample grid shows three scales and four dimensions. This is the most common, but sometimes we use more. Rarely, however, do we go over our maximum of five scale levels and six to seven dimensions.

In this chapter, we will look at the four component parts of the rubric and, using an oral presentation assignment as an example, develop the previous grid *part-by-part* until it is a useful grading tool (a usable rubric) for the professor and a clear indication of expectations and actual performance for the student.

Part-by-Part Development of a Rubric

Part 1: Task Description

The task description is almost always originally framed by the instructor and involves a "performance" of some sort by the student. The task can take the form of a specific assignment, such as a paper, a poster, or a presentation. The task can also apply to overall behavior, such as participation, use of proper lab protocols, and behavioral expectations in the classroom.

We place the task description, usually cut and pasted from the syllabus, at the top of the grading rubric, partly to remind ourselves how the assignment was written as we grade, and to have a handy reference later on when we may decide to reuse the same rubric.

More important, however, we find that the task assignment grabs the students' attention in a way nothing else can when placed at the top of what they know will be a grading tool. With the added reference to their grades, the task assignment and the rubric criteria become more immediate to students and are more carefully read. Students focus on grades. Sad, but true. We might as well take advantage of it to communicate our expectations as clearly as possible.

If the assignment is too long to be included in its entirety on the rubric, or if there is some other reason for not including it there, we put the title of the full assignment at the top of the rubric: for example, "Rubric for Oral Presentation." This will at least remind the students that there is a full description elsewhere, and it will facilitate later reference and analysis for the professor. Sometimes we go further and add the words "see syllabus" or "see handout." Another possibility is to put the larger task description along the side of the rubric. For reading and grading ease, rubrics should seldom, if ever, be more than one page long.

Most rubrics will contain both a descriptive title and a task description. Figure 1.2 illustrates Part 1 of our sample rubric with the title and task description highlighted.

Part 2: Scale

The scale describes how well or how poorly any given task has been performed and occupies yet another side of the grid to complete the rubric's evaluative goal. Terms used to describe the level of performance should be tactful but clear. In the generic rubric, words such as *mastery*, *partial mastery*, *progressing*, and *emerging* provide a more positive, active verb description of what is expected next from the student and also mitigate the potential shock of low marks in the lowest levels of the scale. Some professors may prefer to use nonjudgmental, noncompetitive language, such as "high level," "middle level," and "beginning level," whereas others prefer numbers or even grades.

Changing Communities in Our City

Task Description: Each student will make a 5-minute presentation on the changes in one Portland community over the past thirty years. The student may focus the presentation in any way he or she wishes, but there needs to be a thesis of some sort, not just a chronological exposition. The presentation should include appropriate photographs, maps, graphs, and other visual aids for the audience.

	Scale level 1	Scale level 2	Scale level 3
Dimension 1			
Dimension 2			
Dimension 3			
Dimension 4			

Figure 1.2   Part 1: Task description.

Here are some commonly used labels compiled by Huba and Freed (2000, p. 180):

- Sophisticated, competent, partly competent, not yet competent (NSF Synthesis Engineering Education Coalition, 1997)
- Exemplary, proficient, marginal, unacceptable
- Advanced, intermediate high, intermediate, novice (American Council of Teachers of Foreign Languages, 1986, p. 278)
- distinguished, proficient, intermediate, novice (Gotcher, 1997)
- accomplished, average, developing, beginning (College of Education, 1997)

We almost always confine ourselves to three levels of performance when we first construct a rubric. After the rubric has been used on a real assignment, we often expand that to five. It is much easier to refine the descriptions of the assignment and create more levels after seeing what our students actually do.

Changing Communities in Our City

Task Description: Each student will make a 5-minute presentation on the changes in one Portland community over the past thirty years. The student may focus the presentation in any way he or she wishes, but there needs to be a thesis of some sort, not just a chronological exposition. The presentation should include appropriate photographs, maps, graphs, and other visual aids for the audience.

	Excellent	Competent	Needs work
Dimension 1			
Dimension 2			
Dimension 3			
Dimension 4			

Figure 1.3   Part 2: Scale.

Figure 1.3 presents the Part 2 version of our rubric where the scale has been highlighted.

There is no set formula for the number of levels a rubric scale should have. Most professors prefer to clearly describe the performances at three or even five levels using a scale. But five levels is enough. The more levels there are, the more difficult it becomes to differentiate between them and to articulate precisely why one student's work falls into the scale level it does. On the other hand, more specific levels make the task clearer for the student and they reduce the professor's time needed to furnish detailed grading notes. Most professors consider three to be the optimum number of levels on a rubric scale.

If a professor chooses to describe only one level, the rubric is called a holistic rubric or a scoring guide rubric. It usually contains a description of the highest level of performance expected for each dimension, followed by room for scoring and describing in a "Comments" column just how far the student has come toward achieving or not achieving that level. Scoring guide rubrics, however, usually require considerable additional explanation in the form of written notes and so are more time-consuming than grading with a three-to-five-level rubric.

Part 3: Dimensions

The dimensions of a rubric lay out the parts of the task simply and completely. A rubric can also clarify for students how their task can be broken down into components and which of those components are most important. Is it the grammar? The analysis? The factual content? The research techniques? And how much weight is given to each of these aspects of the assignment? Although it is not necessary to weight the different dimensions differently, adding points or percentages to each dimension further emphasizes the relative importance of each aspect of the task.

Dimensions should actually represent the type of component skills students must combine in a successful scholarly work, such as the need for a firm grasp of content, technique, citation, examples, analysis, and a use of language appropriate to the occasion. When well done, the dimensions of a rubric (usually listed along one side of the rubric) will not only outline these component skills, but after the work is graded, they should provide a quick overview of the student's strengths and weaknesses in each dimension.

Dimensions need not and should not include any description of the quality of the performance. "Organization," for example, is a common dimension, but not "Good Organization." We leave the question of the quality of student work within that dimension to the scale and the description of the dimension, as illustrated in Part 4 of the rubric development.

Breaking up the assignment into its distinct dimensions leads to a kind of task analysis with the components of the task clearly identified. Both students and professors find this useful. It tells the student much more than a mere task assignment or a grade reflecting only the finished product. Together with good descriptions, the dimensions of a rubric provide detailed feedback on specific parts of the assignment and how well or poorly those were carried out. This is especially useful in assignments such as our oral presentation example in which many different dimensions come into play, as shown in Figure 1.4, where the dimensions, Part 3 of the rubric, are highlighted.

Part 4: Description of the Dimensions

Dimensions alone are all-encompassing categories, so for each of the dimensions, a rubric should also contain at the very least a description

Changing Communities in Our City

Task Description: Each student will make a 5-minute presentation on the changes in one Portland community over the past thirty years. The student may focus the presentation in any way he or she wishes, but there needs to be a thesis of some sort, not just a chronological exposition. The presentation should include appropriate photographs, maps, graphs, and other visual aids for the audience.

	Excellent	Competent	Needs work
Knowledge/understanding 20%/20 points			
Thinking/inquiry 30%/30 points			
Communication 20%/20 points			
Use of visual aids 20%/20 points			
Presentation skills 10%/10 points			

Figure 1.4 Part 3: Dimensions.

of the highest level of performance in that dimension. A rubric that contains only the description of the highest level of performance is called a scoring guide rubric and is shown in Figure 1.5.

Scoring guide rubrics allow for greater flexibility and the personal touch, but the need to explain in writing where the student has failed to meet the highest levels of performance does increase the time it takes to grade using scoring guide rubrics.

For most tasks, we prefer to use a rubric that contains at least three scales and a description of the most common ways in which students fail to meet the highest level of expectations. Figure 1.6 illustrates the rubric with three levels on the scale that was actually used for grading the "Changing Communities in Our City" assignment. Note how the next level down on the scale indicates the difference between that level of performance and the ideal, whereas the last level places the

Changing Communities in Our City

Task Description: Each student will make a 5-minute presentation on the changes in one Portland community over the past thirty years. The student may focus the presentation in any way he or she wishes, but there needs to be a thesis of some sort, not just a chronological exposition. The presentation should include appropriate photographs, maps, graphs, and other visual aids for the audience.

	Criteria	Comments	Points
Knowledge/ understanding 20%	The presentation demonstrates a depth of historical understanding by using relevant and accurate detail to support the student's thesis. Research is thorough and goes beyond what was presented in class or in the assigned texts.		
Thinking/ inquiry 30%	The presentation is centered around a thesis, which shows a highly developed awareness of historiographic or social issues and a high level of conceptual ability.		
Communication 20%	The presentation is imaginative and effective in conveying ideas to the audience. The presenter responds effectively to audience reactions and questions.		
Use of visual aids 20%	The presentation includes appropriate and easily understood visual aids, which the presenter refers to and explains at appropriate moments in the presentation.		
Presentation skills 10%	The presenter speaks clearly and loudly enough to be heard, using eye contact, a lively tone, gestures, and body language to engage the audience.		

Figure 1.5   Part 4: Scoring guide rubric: Description of dimensions at highest level of performance.

Changing Communities in Our City

Task Description: Each student will make a 5-minute presentation on the changes in one Portland community over the past thirty years. The student may focus the presentation in any way he or she wishes, but there needs to be a thesis of some sort, not just a chronological exposition. The presentation should include appropriate photographs, maps, graphs, and other visual aids for the audience.

	Excellent	Competent	Needs work
Knowledge/ understanding 20%	The presentation demonstrates a depth of historical understanding by using relevant and accurate detail to support the student's thesis. Research is thorough and goes beyond what was presented in class or in the assigned texts.	The presentation uses knowledge that is generally accurate with only minor inaccuracies and that is generally relevant to the student's thesis. Research is adequate but does not go much beyond what was presented in class or in the assigned text.	The presentation uses little relevant or accurate information, not even that which was presented in class or in the assigned texts. Little or no research is apparent.
Thinking/ inquiry 30%	The presentation is centered around a thesis, which shows a highly developed awareness of historiographic or social issues and a high level of conceptual ability.	The presentation shows an analytical structure and a central thesis, but the analysis is not always fully developed or linked to the thesis.	The presentation shows no analytical structure and no central thesis.
Communication 20%	The presentation is imaginative and effective in conveying ideas to the audience. The presenter responds effectively to audience reactions and questions.	Presentation techniques used are effective in conveying main ideas, but they are a bit unimaginative. Some questions from the audience remain unanswered.	The presentation fails to capture the interest of the audience and/or is confusing in what is to be communicated.
Use of visual aids 20%	The presentation includes appropriate and easily understood visual aids, which the presenter refers to and explains at appropriate moments in the presentation.	The presentation includes appropriate visual aids, but these are too few, are in a format that makes them difficult to use or understand, or the presenter does not refer to or explain them in the presentation.	The presentation includes no visual aids or includes visual aids that are inappropriate or too small or messy to be understood. The presenter makes no mention of them in the presentation.
Presentation skills 10%	The presenter speaks clearly and loudly enough to be heard, using eye contact, a lively tone, gestures, and body language to engage the audience.	The presenter speaks clearly and loudly enough to be heard but tends to drone or fails to use eye contact, gestures, and body language consistently or effectively at times.	The presenter cannot be heard or speaks so unclearly that she or he cannot be understood. There is no attempt to engage the audience through eye contact, gestures, or body language.

Figure 1.6 Part 4: Three-level rubric: Description of dimensions with all levels of performance described.

emphasis on what might have been accomplished but was not. This puts the emphasis not on the failure alone, but also on the possibilities. This final rubric emphasizes Part 4 of rubric development for an oral presentation with the descriptions of the dimensions highlighted.

Creating Your First Rubric: Is It Worth the Time and Effort?

Professors who regularly construct and use rubrics can create a rubric like the oral presentation rubric we used as an example in less than an hour, less if they are simply modifying an existing rubric designed for a similar assignment. For beginners, however, the first few rubrics may take more time than they save.

This time is not wasted, however. When we first began constructing and using rubrics, we quickly found that they not only cut down on grading time and provided fuller feedback to our students, but they affected our classroom preparation and instruction as well.

The first step in constructing or adapting any rubric is quite simply a time of reflection, of putting into words basic assumptions and beliefs about teaching, assessment, and scholarship. We put ourselves in the place of our students by recalling our own student days and focusing on not only *what* we learned but *how* we learned it best— that is, what expectations were clear, what assignments were significant, and what feedback was helpful. That reflection translated into classroom practices as we became more adept at imparting not only our knowledge and expectations for each assignment, but what we hoped our students would accomplish through fulfilling the assignments we gave. Further down the road, we realized our students were not like us and our assignments should acknowledge different student learning styles.

We even began to involve our students in developing the rubrics. In so doing, we found that, as Cafferalla and Clark (1999) concluded in their analysis of studies of adult learners, making the process of learning as collaborative as possible for our students resulted in better teaching.

Although the first few rubrics may take considerable time to construct, they do save time in grading, right from the very beginning. When the sample rubric used in this chapter was used in a class of more than thirty students, for example, the time taken to grade the presentations was reduced to the actual class time in which the presentations were given, plus an extra hour or so devoted to adding a few individualized notes to each rubric. We simply circled whatever categories applied during or immediately after the student presented. Aside from saving time, this meant that the grades and comments were handed back to the students the very next class period, while the memory of the assignment was fresh in their minds. Timely feedback means more student learning.

Rubrics not only save time in the long run, but they are also valuable pedagogical tools because they make us more aware of our individual teaching styles and methods, allow us to impart more clearly our intentions and expectations, and provide timely, informative feedback to our students. Chapter 2 elaborates on these reasons for incorporating rubrics into your classroom instructional practices.

2

WHY USE RUBRICS?

Rubrics save time, provide timely, meaningful feedback for students, and have the potential to become an effective part of the teaching and learning process. In fact, the main reason we don't use rubrics more often is simply because most of us have been unaware of them. Rubrics were not part of our own experience as students, and most of us find that we often teach as we were taught.

However, there are many reasons to use rubrics, reasons having to do not only with efficient use of time and sound pedagogy but, moreover, with basic principles of equity and fairness. In this chapter, we will look at the pragmatic, pedagogical, and equitable reasons for using rubrics.

Rubrics Provide Timely Feedback

The timing of feedback can be a vexing point between professors and students. We struggle to grade each assignment fairly and individually; students then complain that work is not handed back soon enough. Sometimes it seems to us as if students don't care as much about quality feedback (detailed feedback they can act on) as they do about getting their work back speedily. Many of us interpret this to mean that all students care about is their final grade. Although this may be at least partly true, Rucker and Thomson's (2003) research on feedback and learning among college students suggests the students' demand for speed may be valid. After studying 104 students in education and communication classes, Rucker and Thomson concluded that time actually was a factor in making feedback meaningful and useful to students. Feedback was most effective when given as soon as possible after task completion in helping students make positive changes in their subsequent work. Taras's (2003) work with British undergraduates also noted the importance of feedback both for learning and for developing personal habits of self-assessment. Ilgen, Peterson, Martin, and Boeschen's (1981) classic work went further to note an actual decline in the value of feedback as time between it and the task increased: "The longer the delay in the receipt of feedback, the less the effect of feedback on performance" (p. 354). Extensive research over the years has validated that feedback, especially timely feedback, facilitates learning (Black & Wiliam, 1998).

But how are we expected to grade 30 research papers in the space of 48 hours so that they can be handed back while the feedback will still do the most good? The answer, of course, is rubrics. Rubrics are wonderful time savers and, for many of us, when first starting to use rubrics, timeliness is the main virtue that justifies their use. Rubrics allow us to meet the deadline posed by student attention spans and expectations and to do it without sacrificing the need for that feedback to be detailed and specific to each student's individual case.

As many of us know, most students make the same or similar mistakes on any given assignment. The combination of mistakes may be different and individual, but the actual mistakes are much the same. As a result, when we seriously try to offer specific, individual feedback to each student in note form, we often find ourselves writing variations on the same themes on most of the papers.

A rubric eliminates this problem. In a rubric, we simply incorporate easily predictable notes into the "descriptions of dimensions" portion of the rubric. Then, when grading time comes, all we need do is circle or check off all comments that apply to each specific student and perhaps add a note here and there where the rubric does not cover what was done precisely enough, where added emphasis is needed, or where the connection between one or more aspects of the student's performance needs to be stressed. The use of the rubric does not, of course, preclude notes specific to the student that can be placed on the rubric, the paper itself, or elsewhere. The evaluative process of grading remains the same, as does the specificity of the feedback, but the time taken to transmit the feedback to the student is cut by at least 50% and often more.

The result is an easier grading process for us, and timely, detailed, often easier-to-read feedback for the student.

Rubrics Prepare Students to Use Detailed Feedback

It's a vicious cycle. Students *say* they want detailed feedback so that they can know what they are doing right so they can keep doing it, as well as what they are doing wrong so that they can improve.

Yet, as we often discover, students barely seem to read, let alone absorb, the extended notes on their work that took up so much of our grading time. In time, some of us may become discouraged and stop writing such detailed notes. If this continues, eventually we may find that our written comments are confined to terse statements such as "lacks cohesion, needs more references, organized, C+."

Students are understandably confused and discouraged by such laconic remarks, and here too, research bears them out. Brinko (1993) found that feedback was most effective when it contained as much information as possible rather than simply evaluating the level of the work. The same study revealed, however, that including a description of the highest level of achievement possible was also useful to students. Balancing these two findings is where rubrics excel.

The demand for an explanation of the highest level of achievement possible and detailed feedback is fulfilled in the rubric itself. The highest level descriptions of the dimensions are, in fact, the highest level of achievement possible, whereas the remaining levels, circled or checked off, are typed versions of the notes we regularly write on student work explaining how and where they failed to meet that highest level. The student still receives all the necessary details about how and where the assignment did or did not achieve its goal, and even suggestions (in the form of the higher levels of descriptions) as to how it might have been done better.

Moreover, because we discuss the rubric and thereby the grading criteria in class, the student has a much better idea of what these details mean. Even when we make extensive notes and students actually do read them, there can still be quite a gap between comments and student understanding of expectations. For example, students may not have been acquainted with terms such as *context, analysis,* or *citations* before the rubric discussion began, but by the time they receive their graded work back, such words should have clear meaning for them.

Rubrics can also come to the rescue when students ask for serious help on specific, ongoing problems in their class work. In this case, we have to try to determine if their work is improving overall. Except for numbers or letter grades in the grade book, we have found that we have little idea whether and how a student's individual work may or may not be improving over time, still less in what ways. So we ask the student to bring in all work done to date, preferably the copies with the grading notes on them. All too often, we discover the student has not saved those notes or even the work. Neither have we.

Students are, of course, no more likely to keep completed rubrics than they are to keep complete collections of their other graded work. This is why some of us keep rubrics separate from the actual work until we have had a chance to run the rubrics through a copy machine. Only later is the original rubric stapled to the assignment to be handed back. In this way, we are able to keep a complete record of each student's progress without much extra effort. Moreover, the detailed feedback on the rubric becomes a useful tool for analyzing precisely where a student's strengths and weaknesses lie.

Using rubrics for overall assessment as well as immediate grading meets the demand for greater detail in feedback and also for determining whether a student's work is actually improving over time. A quick scan across several rubrics can even provide detailed information about the dimensions in which a student's work is improving and is not improving. Moreover, because many of us are likely to use similar formats and dimensions in constructing rubrics, the accumulated record is easy to read for both of us. Laid side by side, three or more rubrics usually reveal a pattern over time. For example, if "Organization" is a dimension on several rubrics and the student continually gets low marks in that area, we immediately know where to start in giving meaningful, useful advice and suggestions.

Students are often surprised to realize that they are receiving the same levels of commentary in the same dimensions with great regularity. Such students might, of course, have also noticed that they were receiving the same comments in written notes, but the grid pattern of the rubric, with its clearly defined dimensions, makes doubly clear which areas need work. If a student is taking classes from more than one professor who uses rubrics, the pattern may become even clearer.

Using several rubrics of completed assignments, students can draw their own conclusions about the weaknesses in their work and set out their own plans for improvement as well. As Huba and Freed (2000) have pointed out, this is the ideal way that motivation develops and learning occurs: "Feedback that focuses on self-assessment and self-improvement is a form of intrinsic motivation" (p. 59). Once students clearly see how to improve, they can focus on that. Then the rubric comparisons of student performance over time may begin to reflect a more cheerful pattern of steady improvement.

Rubrics Encourage Critical Thinking

Because of the rubric format, students may notice for themselves the patterns of recurring problems or ongoing improvement in their work, and this self-discovery is one of the happiest outcomes of using rubrics. By encouraging students to think critically about their own learning, rubrics can inspire precisely the pattern of "self-assessment and self-improvement" intrinsic to creating the kind of motivated, creative students we all want in our classes. Used in conjunction with good academic advising, rubrics can play a major role in contributing to students' development of a more scholarly form of critical thinking—that is, the ability to think, reason, and make judgments based on an independent, accurate accumulation of data and an open-minded approach to each new topic (Huba & Freed, 2000).

We all want students who demonstrate such traits. Most of us hope that our classes, regardless of discipline, will contribute to producing such habits of thinking and learning. We also know that students need to be challenged to think critically, and we know what kinds of assignments will lead to critical thinking in our respective disciplines. Yet research shows that many of us continue to give too many of the multiple-choice tests and short-answer writing assignments that we know produce mostly rote memory skills and low-level, unconnected thinking (Boud, 1990; Huba & Freed, 2000). A major issue here is time constraints imposed by the need to grade the results. Using rubrics speeds up grading time enormously, thus allowing us to assign more complex tasks leading to critical thinking. However, that is not the limit of what rubrics can do toward promoting greater emphasis on critical thinking.

The greatest way that rubrics begin to promote scholarly critical thinking is in the classroom discussion of the rubric prior to the students beginning the assignment. Many of the rubric's dimensions break down the components of critical thinking in an explicit manner, while the descriptions of those dimensions spell out explicit demands for the basic components of critical thinking. These usually include such basics as the inclusion of an independent thesis, supporting data that is accurate and relevant, thought processes and analyses that are clearly shown, and judgments based on an open-minded consideration of all of these components. For most professors, these demands are so basic that they are often left implicit in the assignment and so may be overlooked by the students until the assignment is complete. By passing out the rubric in advance and allowing time for these components to be discussed, we make our implicit expectations explicit. In discussing the rubric, we are modeling, in reverse, the criteria by which the work will be graded and also the elements of critical thinking that are important in almost every scholarly work in almost any discipline.

Not all components of a rubric relate equally to critical thinking, of course. Punctuality, grammar and spelling, and other technical skills can and do affect communication and therefore grading but are not themselves evidence of scholarly critical thinking. If we want our students to understand that some dimensions are far more important than others, we can communicate that on the rubric by assigning points or percentages according to importance of that dimension to the final product. For example, on the 100-point paper illustrated in Chapter 1, the dimension "Communication" got 20 percent (or 20 points) of the grade, whereas "Presentation skills" got only 10 percent (or 10 points) of the final grade and "Thinking/inquiry" pulled a whopping 30 percent (or 30 points) of the final grade. By including points that make it clear that those components that relate to critical thinking are worth more in the overall grade than the technical skills, a rubric communicates what is important in scholarship in a direct and visual way. Further classroom discussion of the meaning of these critical thinking components can also clarify and explain the habits of mind we expect our students to demonstrate not only for a given assignment or class, but throughout their college careers and, for that matter, the rest of their lives.

Rubrics Facilitate Communication With Others

Whether we think about it that way or not, most of us teach in collaboration with others. The most common "others" in our academic teaching life are usually teaching assistants of some sort. Other significant groups involved in teaching our students may include the staff of a university writing center, tutors or remedial teaching staff, adjunct, and every other professor from whom those students are learning. Rubrics allow us to communicate our goals and intentions to all these people, sometimes without us even being aware that communication is taking place.

Teaching assistants (T.A.s) are the most obvious "other" people involved with our teaching, particularly if they lead discussion or lab sections for the class or grade papers. Rubrics tell the T.A. directly and clearly what we expect from the students; what they should be focusing on in the small group work, the lab, or the seminar; and what grading criteria we have in mind. Sometimes it is useful to involve T.A.s in the construction of the rubric from the start, as T.A.s often have a clearer idea of the individual students' needs and level of comprehension (see Chapter 5 for a discussion of rubric construction with T.A.s and others). Moreover, because many T.A.s plan to become professors in the future, modeling the use of rubrics can affect their teaching practices later on.

Another group who can benefit from our use of a rubric are those who assist students with specific learning problems. The most common of these teaching collaborators is the staff of the writing center. As anyone who has ever worked in a writing center knows, students who are having the most serious problems with their writing are often the last people who can explain the details of the assignment; often the reason they are at the writing center is because they have problems communicating. Much of the time, the writing center staff wind up calling the professor simply to be sure they are not leading the student in the wrong direction. If the student arrives at the center with a rubric, however, the task assignment and expectations are right in front of the person working in the writing center, and most writing center staff members can easily decode the intent behind the details of the rubric. The same is true of math tutors, language drill leaders, and even computer staff who may be called on to help with analytical programs.

The next group who may find rubrics useful are new faculty and adjunct professors. These newcomers are often less distressed at finding themselves without a desk or a mailbox than they are about finding themselves without a clue about the departmental expectations for the classes they are about to teach. A review of past syllabi will show them the lay of the land and the overview of the content, and it will give them some idea of the assignments. However, a review of past rubrics goes further, showing the new faculty member or adjunct not only the assignments but also the expectations for student performance in the course and in the discipline. Armed with both past syllabi and rubrics, newly arrived faculty can feel they have as good an idea of what led their new department to create the course as they would have had if they had sat in on the original department meetings where the faculty spelled out the reasons for creating the classes they will teach.

The final group of "others" who may benefit from rubrics are professors who are teaching the same class or even the same students. Most of us have little knowledge about what our colleagues do in class, even when those colleagues teach in the same discipline or in related fields. Often this is because many of us value our own autonomy in the classroom and worry about violating that of our colleagues, but the truth is that knowing what is going on in closely related classes can be useful, both in avoiding redundant efforts and in understanding what students are being taught. Within departments, rubrics can be shared to determine whether or not there is consensus on what is being taught at each level, how it is being taught, and why.

Sharing rubrics can also reveal the degree to which grading is consistent. Professors are often startled to find out how consistent their teaching and grading really are. In a recent and local case, Portland State University professors who collaborated on a single rubric for a shared assignment were surprised and reassured to discover that their standards and expectations were not wildly out of line with those of their colleagues. For a few of us, of course, rubrics may reveal that we do grade differently from our colleagues. Rubrics cannot tell us what to do about that, if anything, but they can at least make us aware of the situation.

Rubrics Help Us to Refine Our Teaching Skills

How do we know if we are good teachers? How can we find out what we can do to become better ones? Standardized student evaluations are one source. Yet the questions are often broad and therefore difficult to apply. Moreover, because they can be used in faculty promotion and tenure, most of us are a bit defensive about them. Even in the best of circumstances, these evaluations only reflect the students' responses to items about whether the professor was knowledgeable, an engaging lecturer, or well organized in running the class (Huba & Freed, 2000). Even the evaluations that actually ask students whether or not they learned anything may simply ask for the students' opinions on that topic. They do not provide actual evidence or reveal details of what students may or may not have learned.

In the same way that keeping copies of individual student rubrics can allow us to pinpoint a student's continuing improvement or weaknesses over time, rubrics showing student development over time can also allow us to gain a clearer view of teaching blind spots, omissions, and strengths. If, for example, the majority of students in several classes are showing weak results in the use of citations, this should be a wake-up call to us that we need to be talking more about how and why citations are important. If there is a pattern of problems regarding inadequate use of examples, this too can be pinpointed and corrected. And subsequent rubrics from subsequent classes should provide us with evidence as to whether or not our changed teaching strategies are working. Needless to say, such results can also be used to provide persuasive evidence of teaching improvement in applications for promotion and tenure (see Chapters 6 and 11).

Referencing overall rubric results in class can also be a wonderful way to address class problems without singling out any particular student or group of students. If, for example, fully half the class lost points on the "Reflection" dimension of an essay, perhaps they really do not understand what critical reflection means. Mentioning this as we pass the graded assignments back, and again as we begin the discussion of the next assignment, not only cut down on the number of individual conferences we might otherwise have with students in our office, but it can also allow us to reach the student who is too shy, too insecure, or too unaware of academic survival skills to show up in our offices. Discussing problems that a large number of students share with direct reference to the rubric not only provides a solid rationale for discussing a task after the fact, but also offers students a chance to see how they can and should be using rubrics in evaluating their own performance, preferably before assignments are turned in.

Whatever we choose to do with them, collected rubrics provide a record of the specific details of how students performed on any given task, allowing us to quickly notice and correct any across-the-class blind spots or omissions. They can also provide an unexpected pat on the back as we notice improvements across the board, or perhaps even evidence of teaching areas that need no improvement from the start. And for junior faculty, they can provide that evidence in a form that can be included in portfolios submitted for promotion and tenure.

Rubrics Level the Playing Field

In recent years, the numbers of minority first-generation students coming into universities has increased enormously (American Council on Education, 2001; Mellow, Van Slyck, & Eynon, 2002). Most of us have welcomed the change, noting the benefits of a more diverse student body on the educational experience of all students and the educational benefit for citizens in our democracy. Yet the more diverse student body also presents challenges, as shown by the proliferation of support programs for these students (Anaya & Cole, 2001; Rodriguez, 2003). Most of these support programs, however, deal with issues other than in-class learning, such as English language problems, financial issues, childcare, and time management. All of these issues have an impact on class learning, of course, but issues specific to the classroom experience are left for teachers to deal with.

One issue that is specific to the classroom experience is that of "translation." We do not refer here to the fact that many of these students may have English communication problems, but to the fact that even native speakers of English may not speak the kind of English that is used in academia. In the past, many of our students came from college-educated families where such English was taken for granted or went to preparatory schools where basic academic terminology was used and explained, which led to success in postsecondary institutions (National Center for Educational Statistics, 2002). Now, however, teachers must learn to communicate with students for whom the words we use in daily academic speech are a foreign language or at least a bizarre dialect.

Rubrics can act as wonderful translation devices in this new environment. Not only do they help such students understand what teachers are talking about, but they help teachers understand when and where our words are not being understood or, worse yet, are being completely misunderstood. In discussing papers, for example, we may be startled to discover that many students think "introduction" and "conclusion" are synonyms for "beginning" and "end" or that "critical thinking" means criticizing something. We may also not realize that our students do not understand the difference between a discussion and an argument or between an academic debate and a shout-down match. Similarly, some students may assume that "analysis" refers only to situations in which numbers are involved or to the analyses contained in secondary sources. The revelation that in an academic paper, for example, "analysis" most often means their own conclusions informed by data can be startling to them.

Above all, first-generation students are apt to think of education in terms of the concrete knowledge absorbed. The correct use of rubrics can alter their entire understanding of the task of getting an education by introducing them to whole new concepts such as critical thinking, argumentation, objective and subjective views, and the other academic terms teachers take for granted. Rubrics offer a way for us to pinpoint problems in communication and deal with them until we are sure that our students are actually speaking the same language we are. Then we can communicate our expectations in ways that go beyond merely knowing the content of the class, especially if the rubrics are discussed or even constructed (see Chapter 4) in class.

Such "translation" is not mere hand holding because we cannot always assume that students will be able to figure these things out "on their own." The truth is, they never did it "on their own." Some students arrive with that knowledge already in place because of a privileged upbringing or education. Many of those who are now arriving in our classes lack that privileged past. Failing to address this reality by keeping assignments vague and failing to spell out what we mean by the academic terms we use benefits those who have already had the advantage of growing up in college-educated households or attending preparatory schools. Pretending all students are starting from the same point does not ensure equity in the classroom; it simply privileges those who were privileged already.

Few of us would ignore such inequity deliberately, but we may do so unthinkingly or accidentally. Rubrics certainly are not the only way to address these inequities, nor are they a panacea. However, they can and should be a major component in the ongoing effort to create more equitable classrooms.

Conclusion

Why use rubrics? This chapter provided six key reasons for constructing and using rubrics in our classrooms:

- Rubrics provide timely feedback.
- Rubrics prepare students to use detailed feedback.
- Rubrics encourage critical thinking.
- Rubrics facilitate communication with others.
- Rubrics help us refine our teaching methods.
- Rubrics level the playing field.

The incredibly useful and flexible rubric accomplishes many objectives for our own classes as well as for our students' overall university experience. In the next chapter, we will describe in detail how to construct a rubric from the assignment in our syllabus to its final form.

3

HOW TO CONSTRUCT A RUBRIC

Constructing your first rubric may seem daunting. Time consuming too. In this chapter, we will share some ways to make constructing useful, high-quality rubrics easier and faster.

First, we remind ourselves that rubric construction gets easier with time, partly because we get better at it and also because we often find ourselves revising rubrics we created for other, similar assignments. One shortcut to creating your first rubrics is to adapt the model rubrics provided throughout this book and at http://styluspub.com/resources/introductiontorubrics.aspx to serve your needs.

Second, we break the task down into four key stages. These four stages apply whether you choose to revise an existing rubric or construct your own from scratch.

Four Key Stages in Constructing a Rubric

Whether you choose to construct your own rubric from scratch by yourself, with teaching assistants, with colleagues, or even with students (see Chapters 4 and 5), four basic stages are involved in constructing any rubric regardless of the number of people participating:

Stage 1: Reflecting. In this stage, we take the time to reflect on what we want from the students, why we created this assignment, what happened the last time we gave it, and what our expectations are.

Stage 2: Listing. In this stage, we focus on the particular details of the assignment and what specific learning objectives we hope to see in the completed assignment.

Stage 3: Grouping and Labeling. In this stage, we organize the results of our reflections in Stages 1 and 2, grouping similar expectations together in what will probably become the rubric dimensions.

Stage 4: Application. In this stage, we apply the dimensions and descriptions from Stage 3 to the final form of the rubric, using the grid formats shown in Chapter 1 or in the appendices.

In this chapter, we will show each step in each stage of rubric construction in detail, using examples from both a freshman core course and a graduate seminar. We do this to show how rubrics are drawn from and integral to our overall teaching goals and methods of instruction and to suggest some of the adaptations that may be necessary in different disciplines and at different levels of higher education.

Stage 1: Reflecting

In Stage 1, reflecting, we reflect not only on the assignment but also on the overall course objectives for this particular class. Moon (1999) defines *reflection* simply as a "mental process with purpose and/or outcome" (p. 5). Whether it is called "reflection" or something else, this kind of focused thinking is a part of every discipline. Even though the way we reflect may be different, the purpose is the same. All of us journal, meditate, draw mind maps, create outlines, make lists, analyze data, synthesize results, or engage in any number of personal or professional forms of reflection. All of us reflect prior to beginning a scholarly task such as writing or creating a new lecture or class plan.

Constructing a rubric requires reflection on our overall class objectives, the assignment itself, its purposes, the task objectives, and students' prior knowledge, as well as our own previous experience with this type of assignment. The kind of reflection we all already do is easily adapted to rubric construction.

To begin a fruitful rubric reflection for any level, we have found it useful to focus on eight questions geared toward focusing our minds on what we already know but may never have articulated:

1. *Why did you create this assignment?* Think back to a previous reflective period, the one you engaged in before or as you wrote your syllabus. Is this assignment primarily designed to push the students to absorb as much content knowledge as possible (e.g., an exam), to develop a learning skill such as critical thinking (e.g., a paper or critique), or to involve students in some sort of experiential learning (e.g., a lab, workshop, or performance)?

2. *Have you given this assignment or a similar assignment before?* What happened the last time you gave this or a similar assignment? What questions did the students ask about this assignment before and after they completed it? Were you pleased or displeased with the general result? What particularly satisfactory results can you recall? What particularly disappointing results can you recall? Are there any changes you can make to the task assignment to improve your chances of getting the same satisfactory results and avoiding the same pitfalls?

3. *How does this assignment relate to the rest of what you are teaching?* In what ways does it relate to other assignments? How important is it to the completion of future assignments that students complete this task successfully? How important is it to your discipline or their scholarly lives as a whole that they do well on this assignment?

4. *What skills will students need to have or develop to successfully complete this assignment?* Do they already have such skills and need to develop them further, or are they starting from scratch? Is the class mixed in terms of their existing capabilities? What, if anything, do you want to do about their skill levels? Is demonstrating one or more of these skills more important to you than others?

5. *What exactly is the task assigned?* Does it break down into a variety of different tasks? Are one or more of these component tasks more important than others? How can/will you explain the breakdown and nature of these component tasks to the students?

6. *What evidence can students provide in this assignment that would show they have accomplished what you hoped they would accomplish when you created the assignment?* What different kinds of evidence might students use to demonstrate their knowledge and skills?

7. *What are the highest expectations you have for student performance on this assignment overall?* What does an exemplary product look like?

8. *What is the worst fulfillment of the assignment you can imagine, short of simply not turning it in at all?* Where have students fallen

short on the completion of similar assignments in the past? What are some of the pitfalls you might help your students to avoid this time?

We find it helps to write down the answers to these questions, but whether you do or not, the answers should supply the "big picture"—that is, the context of the assignment in the larger context of the class and your overall objectives. The answers should help you decide what kind of rubric will best serve your needs and the needs of your students. They should also help you decide whether you will construct your rubric from scratch or whether one of your old rubrics or a model rubric from this book or elsewhere can be adapted. These answers should also generate ideas that help you construct a high-quality rubric that communicates your expectations clearly to the students.

Stage 2: Listing

In Stage 2, listing, we turn our attention to describing how to capture the details of this assignment. We ask ourselves what specific learning objectives we hope will be accomplished with the completion of this assignment. (See Appendix B on how to write learning objectives.) The objectives will vary according to the overall course objectives, the nature of the task, the grade level of the students, and our experience in giving and grading this assignment. In particular, the answers to questions 4, 5, and 6 regarding skills required, the exact nature of the task, and the types of evidence of learning are most often our starting point in generating this list.

Whichever questions you choose, the answers can be used to create a new list of the most important (to you) learning objectives you expect students to accomplish by completing the task. As with writing, lecture preparation, or other scholarly tasks, the initial lists are apt to be messy accumulations of half-formed and even repetitious ideas to be refined, reorganized, and probably added to as you progress.

Lists of learning objectives can vary tremendously, even in classes that seem very similar and that are taught by the same professor. In the examples that follow, we have included lists from two rather similar assignments taught by the same professor: oral presentations comparing and contrasting Japanese and American film versions of World

War II. One of these, however, was a group project for a freshman core class designed to promote basic academic skills and interdisciplinary thinking. The other was for individual presentations of a similar topic in a graduate seminar in history. The learning objectives vary because of the different grade and skill level of the students, the different formats of the assignments (group and individual), and the long-term goals of the two classes (skills in the former, content in the latter).

The list of learning objectives for the *freshman core class* looked like the list in Figure 3.1. Note that for freshmen, the emphasis is more on skills than content. As Perry (1970) and others have documented, students do not necessarily come to college with the skills to engage in critical thinking. Most also have limited experience with public speaking, scholarly discussion, or cooperative work. Yet to succeed in higher education, students need these sets of skills (King & Kitchener, 1994; Leamnson, 2002). Many new freshmen core classes like those at Portland State University were, in fact, developed in good part to teach such skills. The list of goals and expectations for this class shown in Figure 3.1 reflects the emphasis on communication and critical thinking skills rather than content.

The list of learning objectives for individual presentations in the *graduate seminar* was quite different, as shown in Figure 3.2.

The second list is undoubtedly more satisfying to the "academic" in all of us, but comparing it to the list for the freshman core serves as a reminder of why this list of learning goals is necessary. The professor who created both lists not only drew on her experiential knowledge of student abilities at different levels, her disciplinary focus, and her theoretical biases within that discipline, but also on her understanding of her department's (history) or program's (Freshman Inquiry) objectives. In making her list, she made the difference crystal clear to herself first, a great asset in making things clear to students and for ensuring that the final rubrics assessed what she hoped her students would learn in each class.

Once the learning goals have been listed, you can add a description of the highest level of performance you expect for each learning goal. These will later contribute to the "Descriptions of Dimensions" on the finished rubric. Like the objectives themselves, these descriptions also articulate the individual, disciplinary, and departmental objectives of

Stage 2: Step 1
Freshman Core List of Learning Objectives

Develop public speaking skills.

Work well together as a group.

Learn to organize data and build a logical argument.

Show an awareness of different points of view including those of the presenters.

Recognize and express individual biases and opinions without letting them dominate or distort the evidence.

Recognize and understand how circumstances and events surrounding the creation of the film affect its nature and content.

Compile and effectively utilize accurate and appropriate evidence to support all points.

Figure 3.1   Stage 2: Listing. Step 1: List learning objectives. List of learning objectives for oral presentation assignment in a freshman core class at Portland State University.

the class. For example, Figure 3.3 presents the set of descriptions of the highest level performance of the "Develop public speaking skills" objective for the Freshman Inquiry group project.

There was no similar list of communication skills for the graduate seminar. Graduate students were expected to demonstrate decent communication and critical thinking skills, and these were therefore integrated into more content-focused learning objectives such as the "Tie the film analysis into the overall history and historiography of World War II," as shown in Figure 3.4 on page 37.

Sometimes at this stage, rather than making lists, we use Post-its. The ideas that would have been listed are now separated. We put one idea or performance description on each Post-it. These lists and/or Post-its often wind up stuck all over the office in little clumps of related ideas. The Post-its give us the flexibility to move the ideas around when we begin grouping similar ideas together in the next stage. After listing our writing ideas on Post-its, we color code similar ideas. Color coding helps, although by the end our offices sometimes become so festooned with paper chains that we wonder if the holidays

Stage 2: Step 1
Graduate Seminar List of Learning Objectives

Tie the film analysis into the overall history and historiography of World War II.

Understand and use basic theories of film as presented in the text.

Select or develop a coherent theory to further explore the film in a focused, thematic manner.

Understand how this film compares or contrasts with other films being discussed in this class, especially those we have already seen.

Include and address other critiques of this film, whether to agree or disagree.

Present the results in an organized fashion using whatever visual or audio aids are appropriate and useful for the benefit of the class.

Figure 3.2 Stage 2: Listing. Step 1: List of learning objectives. Learning objectives for an oral presentation in a graduate seminar at Portland State University.

have come early. Cutting and pasting on the computer is tidier and works well for the more virtual minded.

At the end of Stage 2, you will have your overall learning objectives listed for the assignment, and under each objective you will also have a list that describes what the highest performance expectations for that particular learning objective are.

Stage 3: Grouping and Labeling

In Stage 3, grouping and labeling, we group similar performance expectations together and create labels for each group. We start with the final lists of highest performance expectations that we completed in Stage 2. We read through this list of performance expectations carefully and begin to group together items that we think are related. We begin to construct groups of similar performance expectations such as organization, context, analysis, and presentation. This is inevitably a back-and-forth process in which existing groups suggest other groups that make up the overall assignment, while groups, once created, may result in

Stage 2: Step 2
Freshman Core List of Highest Expectations for "Develop Public Speaking Skills" Learning Objective

---

Clear introduction that sets out the thesis and organization of the whole presentation.

Maintains good eye contact.

Body language is expressive and appropriate.

Speaks loudly and slowly enough to be easily understood.

Modulates voice quality and tone appropriately; does not drone.

Uses humor and stories that relate to the topic to liven up presentation.

Does not fumble with the overhead or projector.

Not too many words on the overhead or PowerPoint projection.

Captions of overhead or PowerPoint show key issues and themes.

Handouts are clear.

Handouts show key issues and themes.

Figure 3.3 Stage 2: Listing. Step 2: List of highest expectations. List of highest expectations for public speaking skills learning objective in a freshman inquiry class at Portland State University.

ideas that went together under learning goals being reassigned to different groups. We often find that some performance expectations do not neatly fit in one group. When this happens to us, we construct an entirely new group of these related performance expectations.

Once the performance descriptions are in groups of similar skills, we read them and start to find out what is common across the group and label it. These labels will ultimately become our dimensions on the rubric, so it is important to keep them clear and neutral. We try to limit them to a single word, such as "Organization," "Analysis," or "Citations."

In the case of the freshman core rubric, for example, most of the performance expectations listed in the "Develop public speaking skills" objective were grouped together in a category labeled "Presentation." However, the need for clear overheads, PowerPoints, or handouts also found their way into the "Organization" category because caption

Stage 2: Step 2
Graduate Seminar List of Highest Expectations for "Tie the Film Analysis into the Overall History and Historiography of World War II" Learning Objective

The major historical issue (s) addressed by the film are recognized and clearly articulated.

All major scholarly theories regarding this issue are articulated and the speaker takes a stand one way or another.

The speaker makes it clear what theories most affected her or his approach to the film.

The data introduced are accurate, appropriate, and, if controversial, defended.

Figure 3.4 Stage 2: Listing. Step 2: List of highest expectations. List of highest expectations for the history and historiography learning goal for an oral presentation in a graduate seminar at Portland State University.

selection and other aspects of creating visual aids involve developing an organizational framework. The need for a clear introduction that sets the thesis for the whole presentation might also have gone into the "Organization" category, but in the end it was considered sufficiently important to merit a group of its own labeled "Introduction." Thus, the original list of public speaking skills for the freshman core class wound up in three different groups as shown in Figure 3.5.

At the end of Stage 3, you will have all of the performance expectations related to your learning objectives now regrouped into new groups with labels. The original learning objectives, of course, will be hidden in your rubric but expressed through the individual descriptions of the performance expectations. The performance expectations related to each learning objective will have been separated into more familiar component skills such as "Organization," "Presentation," and "Introduction," which will become the dimensions of your new rubric.

Stage 4: Application

In Stage 4: Application, we transfer our lists and groupings to a rubric grid. The labels for the groups of performance expectations now become the dimensions of the rubric and are placed in the left

Stage 2: Step 2
Freshman Core List of Highest Expectations for "Develop Public Speaking Skills" Learning Objective

Clear introduction that sets out the thesis and organization of the whole presentation.

Maintains good eye contact.

Body language is expressive and appropriate.

Speaks loudly and slowly enough to be easily understood.

Modulates voice quality and tone appropriately: does not drone.

Uses humor and stories that relate to the topic to liven up presentation.

Does not fumble with the overhead or projector.

Not too many words on the overhead or PowerPoint projection.

Captions on overhead or PowerPoint show key issues and themes

Group (Dimension) 1: Presentation

Maintains good eye contact.
Body language is expressive and appropriate.
Speaks loudly and slowly enough to be easily understood.
Modulates voice quality and tone appropriately.
Does not fumble with the overhead or projector.

Group (Dimension) 2: Organization

Captions of overhead or PowerPoint show key issues and themes.
Handouts are clear.
Handouts show key issues and themes.
Uses humor and stories that relate to the topic to illustrate, support, and liven up presentation.

Group (Dimension) 3: Introduction

Clear introduction that sets out the thesis and organization of the whole presentation.

Figure 3.5   Stage 3: Grouping and Labeling. List of highest expectations moved into three groups that become rubric dimensions.

column of the rubric grid, while many of our earlier lists of learning and task objectives find their way into the descriptions of the highest level of performance for each dimension. In the case of the graduate seminar, the process stopped there with the creation of a scoring guide rubric.

Construction of a Scoring Guide Rubric

In the case of the graduate seminar described earlier, the professor decided to create a scoring guide rubric rather than a three- to five-level rubric. A scoring guide rubric lists only one set of criteria: the highest possible performance for each category. Individualized notes then tell students how completely they did or did not meet that criterion. Scoring guide rubrics require more grading time than three- to five-level rubrics, but they are still faster to use for feedback than handwritten notes because we can reference what was left out without having to rewrite it each and every time. Scoring guide rubrics work best for assignments in which students are allowed greater flexibility of approach; in this case, they had the option of focusing on film theory or historical theory. For this reason, these theoretical frameworks were grouped together under the "Context" category, although they had originally been quite separate in terms of learning goals. The need to discuss the historical issues addressed by the film (it was a history class, after all), regardless of the theoretical approach, found its way into both the "Introduction" category and the "Evidence" dimension.

Scoring guide rubrics provide greater flexibility of response and can make grading something that is happening rapidly (like an oral presentation) more organized and easier and quicker to grade when the work is good; they therefore fulfill most of the highest expectations spelled out in the scoring guide rubric. Scoring guide rubrics do not, however, save much time when dealing with a student who has to be given more explicit feedback to be successful the next time (see Chapter 6 on grading using scoring guide rubrics). Of course, sometimes just a simple "see me" encourages the student to seek the more elaborate feedback from the professor. Figure 3.6 illustrates the finished scoring guide rubric used to grade the graduate seminar presentations.

Construction of a Three- to Five-Level Rubric

Unlike the graduate students in the seminar, the professor decided that the students in the freshman class needed a clearer description of what constituted less than exemplary performances, partly in order to know what to avoid and partly to allow her to avoid lengthy written notes. She therefore decided on a three-level rubric with check boxes. A rubric with check boxes simply means breaking down the descriptions of dimensions into individual parts and including a box (□) to check off beside each; this allows us to more accurately pinpoint strengths and weaknesses and show the student how he or she may actually incorporate bits of all three levels in one dimension.

As we noted in Chapter 1, labeling the levels on the scale can be a delicate matter. We need to be clear about expectations and about failures as well as successes, yet we also try to avoid overly negative

Scoring Guide Rubric for Film Presentations

Task Description: Each student will develop an hour-long presentation on a Japanese or American movie about World War II designed to acquaint the class more fully with the theoretical, historical, and interpretive issues surrounding the film. Clips or other audio-visual aids may be used, but guard against overusing these items; remember that we have all seen the movie once.

Film:

	Criteria	Comments
Introduction	The introduction tells the audience exactly what to expect in terms of how the speaker feels about the movie, what theories and theoretical framework(s) she or he will introduce and what conclusions she or he will draw.	
Organization	The presentation is organized to create a logical argument and so that topics that need to be discussed together are presented together.	
Context	The presenter discusses the main historical issues raised by the film and how other film scholars and historians have dealt with these issues both with regard to this film and in general. The presenter explains where he or she stands on these issues, which theories he or she finds most useful, and why.	
Evidence	The presenter includes sufficient, detailed examples from the film and other sources to support her or his analyses.	
Analysis	The presenter uses her or his evidence to support a consistent, coherent analysis of how the film does or does not contribute to our understanding of World War II.	
Presentation	The presenter spoke clearly, slowly, loudly enough to be heard, but not too loudly; used appropriate, effective gestures and body language; and maintained eye contact with the class. Audio-visual aids, if used, are technically sound (to prevent fumbling with equipment), appropriate, and referenced in the presentation.	

Figure 3.6 Stage 4: Application. Groups placed on a scoring guide rubric listing only highest level of expectations for an oral presentation

or competitive labels. These can discourage students. We have found that the best way to avoid overly negative scale labels is to remember that one major purpose of our rubric is to demonstrate for our students the steps toward an exemplary performance. In the case of the three-level rubric for the Freshman Inquiry group project, the professor considered the following options:

- Exemplary, competent, beginning
- Proficient, intermediate, novice
- Exemplary, competent, not yet competent
- Excellent, good, developing
- 1, 2, 3
- Strong, satisfactory, weak

Eventually she settled on "Exemplary," "Competent," and "Developing" as the labels for each level of performance and placed these on the horizontal upper bar of the grid. Then, using her lists and groups from Stage 3, grouping and labeling, she added the "Dimensions" to the vertical side of the grid. Finally, she inserted the descriptions of the highest level of performance in each dimension to the appropriate place in the "Exemplary" column of the grid. The initial grid is shown in Figure 3.7.

To complete the grid and the descriptions of the other levels, we find it easiest to fill in the lowest performance descriptions next. Because they are the lowest task expectations, these descriptions are often simply the negation of the exemplary task description; in this case, we can actually cut and paste the exemplary description and then edit it accordingly. In other cases, however, the lowest performance description is not a direct opposite, but a list of the typical mistakes that we have seen students commit over the years. It is sadly easy to define a very low performance.

This was certainly the case with the Freshman Inquiry rubric. In fact, it looked like Figure 3.8 on page 43, once the "Developing" descriptions of each dimension were filled in.

Once this was done, filling in the middle level became a matter of distinguishing between the two; this is a bit more difficult when working with more levels, but even then, we have found that working

Rubric for Film Presentation

Task Description: Working in groups of four or five, students will develop and present to the class an analysis of a Japanese movie about World War II. This analysis should go beyond a simple synopsis of the movie to discuss how well or poorly the film reflects a particular point of view about the war. You are expected to do additional research to develop this presentation and to use visual aids of some sort. All group members are expected to participate in the presentation.

	Exemplary	Competent	Developing
Individual presentations	❏ The presenter spoke clearly, slowly, and loudly enough to be heard without shouting, and modulated voice tone and quality. ❏ The presenter used expressive, appropriate body language and maintained eye contact with the audience. ❏ The presenter used all the time allotted but did not speak too long. ❏ The presenter used humor and anecdotes appropriately to liven up and illustrate the presentation. ❏ The presenter or an assistant competently handled the equipment.		
Group work	❏ The presentation allowed each member an equal opportunity to shine. ❏ The individual presentations followed one another in a way that promoted a logical discussion of the topic, and connections between individual presentations were clearly shown. ❏ Group members treated each other with courtesy and respect. ❏ The technologies used to illustrate and assist the presentation were appropriate and competently handled without any fumbling.		
Introduction	❏ The thesis is clearly stated at the beginning and carried through in the rest of the presentation. ❏ The topics to be covered are introduced and the direction the overall presentation will take is made clear.		
Individual organization	❏ The individual presentation was well organized in itself with an introduction, body, and conclusion. ❏ That organization was emphasized and made clear to the audience through the use of appropriately captioned PowerPoints, overheads, or handouts.		
Individual content	❏ Facts and examples were detailed, accurate, and appropriate. ❏ Theories referenced were accurately described and appropriately used. ❏ Analyses, discussions, and conclusions were explicitly linked to examples, facts, and theories.		

Figure 3.7   Three-level rubric with check boxes. The scales have been defined and the description of the highest level of performance for each dimension has been filled in.

Rubric for Film Presentation

Task Description: Working in groups of four or five, students will develop and present to the class an analysis of a Japanese movie about World War II. This analysis should go beyond a simple synopsis of the movie to discuss how well or poorly the film reflects a particular point of view about the war. You are expected to do additional research to develop this presentation and to use visual aids of some sort. All group members are expected to participate in the presentation.

	Exemplary	Competent	Developing
Individual presentations	❑ The presenter spoke clearly, slowly, and loudly enough to be heard without shouting, and modulated voice tone and quality. ❑ The presenter used expressive, appropriate body language and maintained eye contact with the audience. ❑ The presenter used all the time allotted but did not speak too long. ❑ The presenter used humor and anecdotes appropriately to liven up and illustrate the presentation. ❑ The presenter or an assistant competently handled the equipment.		❑ The presenter mumbled, spoke too fast or too slow, whispered or shouted, or droned to the point where intelligibility was compromised. ❑ The presenter fidgeted, remained rigid, never looked at the audience, or engaged in other body language that distracted seriously from the content. ❑ The presenter barely used the time allotted or used much too much time. ❑ The lack of humor and anecdotes made the presentation dull. ❑ There was a lot of fumbling with the equipment that could have been prevented with a little practice.
Group work	❑ The presentation allowed each member an equal opportunity to shine. ❑ The individual presentations followed one another in a way that promoted a logical discussion of the topic, and connections between individual presentations were clearly shown. ❑ Group members treated each other with courtesy and respect. ❑ The technologies used to illustrate and assist the presentation were appropriate and competently handled without any fumbling.		❑ The presentation was seriously unbalanced so that one or a few people dominated or carried the ball. ❑ There was little if any evident logic in how the individual presentations followed one another, and the connections between individual presentations were unclear. ❑ Group members showed little respect or courtesy toward one another. ❑ The technologies used to illustrate and assist the presentation were unnecessary, clumsy, and accompanied by too much fumbling with the equipment.
Introduction	❑ The thesis is clearly stated at the beginning and carried through in the rest of the presentation. ❑ The topics to be covered are introduced and the direction the overall presentation will take is made clear.		❑ The thesis is unclear, unstated, and not evident in the rest of the presentation, which is about something else. ❑ There is no indication of what topics will be covered or what direction that coverage will take.
Individual organization	❑ The individual presentation was well organized in itself with an introduction, body, and conclusion. ❑ That organization was emphasized and made clear to the audience through the use of appropriately captioned PowerPoints, overheads, or handouts.		❑ The presentation rambled with little evidence of an introduction, body, or conclusion. ❑ PowerPoints, overheads, or handouts either were not used or did not assist the audience in following the organization in any significant way.
Individual content	❑ Facts and examples were detailed, accurate, and appropriate. ❑ Theories referenced were accurately described and appropriately used. ❑ Analyses, discussions, and conclusions were explicitly linked to examples, facts, and theories.		❑ Facts and examples were seriously lacking in detail, inaccurate, or inappropriate. ❑ Theories referenced were inaccurately described and inappropriately used or not referenced or used at all. ❑ There is no clear connection between analyses, discussions, and examples, facts, and theories.

Figure 3.8 Three-level rubric with check boxes. The descriptions of the highest and lowest levels of performance for each dimension have been filled in.

Rubric for Film Presentation

Task Description: Working in groups of four or five, students will develop and present to the class an analysis of a Japanese movie about World War II. This analysis should go beyond a simple synopsis of the movie to discuss how well or poorly the film reflects a particular point of view about the war. You are expected to do additional research to develop this presentation and to use visual aids of some sort. All group members are expected to participate in the presentation.

	Exemplary	Competent	Developing
Individual presentations	❏ The presenter spoke clearly, slowly, and loudly enough to be heard without shouting, and modulated voice tone and quality. ❏ The presenter used expressive, appropriate body language and maintained eye contact with the audience. ❏ The presenter used all the time allotted but did not speak too long. ❏ The presenter used humor and anecdotes appropriately to liven up and illustrate the presentation.	❏ The presenter was understood but mumbled, spoke too fast or too slow, whispered, shouted, or droned; intelligibility, however, was not compromised. ❏ The presenter's body language did not distract significantly, but the presenter fidgeted, remained rigid, never looked at the audience, or engaged in other inappropriate body language. ❏ The presenter's timing was too long or too brief. ❏ Humor and anecdotes were used, but they were over- or underused to liven up or illustrate the presentation. ❏ Equipment was used but there was some fumbling although not to the point where it seriously distracted from the presentation.	❏ The presenter mumbled, spoke too fast or too slow, whispered or shouted, or droned to the point where intelligibility was compromised. ❏ The presenter fidgeted, remained rigid, never looked at the audience, or engaged in other body language that distracted seriously from the content. ❏ The presenter barely used the time allotted or used much too much time. ❏ The lack of humor and anecdotes made the presentation dull. ❏ There was a lot of fumbling with the equipment that could have been prevented with a little practice.
Group work	❏ The presenter or an assistant competently handled the equipment. ❏ The presentation allowed each member an equal opportunity to shine. ❏ The individual presentations followed one another in a way that promoted a logical discussion of the topic, and connections between individual presentations were clearly shown. ❏ Group members treated each other with courtesy and respect. ❏ The technologies used to illustrate and assist the presentation were appropriate and competently handled without any fumbling.	❏ The presentation was unbalanced in the way time or content was assigned to members. ❏ The individual presentations followed one another in a way that mostly promoted a logical discussion of the topic, but connections between individual presentations were not clearly shown, or the presentation lost direction from time to time for other reasons. ❏ Group members mostly treated each other with courtesy and respect, but there were lapses where members were not listening to each other. ❏ Technologies were used to illustrate and assist the presentation; however, some were off topic, unnecessary, or accompanied by too much fumbling.	❏ The presentation was seriously unbalanced so that one or a few people dominated or carried the ball. ❏ There was little if any evident logic in how the individual presentations followed one another, and the connections between individual presentations were unclear. ❏ Group members showed little respect or courtesy toward one another. ❏ The technologies used to illustrate and assist the presentation were unnecessary, clumsy, and accompanied by too much fumbling.

Figure 3.9   Three-level rubric. All descriptions of dimensions completed.

	Exemplary	Competent	Developing
Introduction	❏ The thesis is clearly stated at the beginning and carried through in the rest of the presentation. ❏ The topics to be covered are introduced and the direction the overall presentation will take is made clear.	❏ The thesis emerges from the presentation but is either unclear, unstated, or not stated directly. ❏ A clear thesis is stated, but it is not carried through in the presentation. ❏ Topics to be covered and the direction the presentation will take are stated, but they are not the topics covered or the direction actually taken.	❏ The thesis is unclear, unstated, and not evident in the rest of the presentation, which is about something else. ❏ There is no indication of what topics will be covered or what direction that coverage will take.
Individual organization	❏ The individual presentation was well organized in itself with an introduction, body, and conclusion. ❏ That organization was emphasized and made clear to the audience through the use of appropriately captioned PowerPoints, overheads, or handouts.	❏ The individual presentation was mostly well organized, but there were problems with the introduction, body, or conclusion. ❏ The presenter used PowerPoints, overheads, or handouts, but these were too wordy or too vague to help the audience follow the organization.	❏ The presentation rambled with little evidence of an introduction, body, or conclusion. ❏ PowerPoints, overheads, or handouts either were not used or did not assist the audience in following the organization in any significant way.
Individual content	❏ Facts and examples were detailed, accurate, and appropriate. ❏ Theories referenced were accurately described and appropriately used. ❏ Analyses, discussions, and conclusions were explicitly linked to examples, facts, and theories.	❏ Facts and examples were mostly detailed, accurate, and appropriate, but there were lapses. ❏ Theories were referenced but they were either not accurately described or not appropriately used. ❏ The connection between analyses, discussions, and conclusions is evident or implied, but it is not explicitly linked to examples, facts, and theories.	❏ Facts and examples were seriously lacking in detail, inaccurate, or inappropriate. ❏ Theories referenced were inaccurately described and inappropriately used or not referenced or used at all. ❏ There is no clear connection between analyses, discussions, and examples, facts, and theories.

Figure 3.9 *Continued*

from the outside in is the best method. Three-level rubrics are relatively easy to construct. The middle level usually contains elements of both sides and some statements of degree of success or achievement. For example, in the Freshman Inquiry group presentation rubric, the professor differentiated between lapses that affected comprehensibility and those that did not. The result is shown in Figure 3.9.

Conclusion

Constructing rubrics using this four-stage approach does not require learning any new skills or procedures. It simply systematizes how we use the skills and talents that made us academics in the first place, from reflecting to listing to categorizing and applying. The use of these skills helps us create a grading tool, the rubric, that is advantageous to both teachers and students. By using the stages in this chapter, we can eventually streamline the process of rubric creation.

As is the case with creating syllabi and other teaching tools, most of us find that after constructing our first few rubrics, we begin to see that what initially seemed a time-consuming addition to our schedules becomes a real time-saver. In addition, we recognize that rubrics help us give more feedback, more consistently, with many more opportunities for all students to not only understand but to meet our expectations. In Chapter 4, we discuss the benefits and challenges of including others in this rubric construction process.

PART II

RUBRIC CONSTRUCTION AND USE IN DIFFERENT CONTEXTS

4

RUBRIC CONSTRUCTION
AND THE CLASSROOM

"Let the students create their own grading tool?" a curmudgeonly friend of ours once sneered. "While you're at it, why not put the fox in charge of the henhouse?" It does sound risky, doesn't it? But with our basic models, described in this chapter, involving students in rubric construction can be safe and highly rewarding for all concerned. In fact, the stages and steps of rubric construction described in Chapter 3 remain much the same regardless of whether you create your rubrics alone in the privacy of your office or in the classroom with the full input of your students.

This chapter introduces five models of how rubric construction can be integrated into classroom teaching, beginning with the rubric you create alone and ending with a model in which the teacher creates the assignment and the students create the rubric, working together in groups.

Involving Students in Rubric Construction

There are three good reasons for integrating rubric construction into classroom teaching:

- It prevents misunderstandings and misinterpretations before they affect student work; this makes for happier students and happier graders.

- It increases student awareness of themselves as "stakeholders" in the educational process, which, in turn, results in greater student involvement in the tasks assigned and greater professionalism and creativity (Boud, 1990; Lewis, Berghoff, & Pheeney, 1999).

- It can actually cut down your workload by letting your students do some of it—that is, create part of their own assessment tool.

Going further depends on your comfort with relinquishing some control over the construction of your grading tool, the rubric, and such instructional considerations as the class level, the objectives of the assignment, the importance of the assignment, and the amount of class time you want to devote to it. Students can always be involved in rubric construction, even if you limit that involvement to having them read and discuss a finished rubric before they begin the assignment.

An application to avoid is what we call the "surprise" rubric. Surprise rubrics happen when we grade an assignment with a rubric that students have never seen before, and then hand back the graded assignment with the rubric attached. When this occurs, students are justifiably miffed. "If you knew what you wanted, why didn't you tell us in the first place?" they ask testily. It is easy to fall into the trap of a "surprise" if we assume that students will automatically know the criteria based on what we say in class, write in the syllabus, and specify in the assignment. Students really want to see the criteria used for grading. Always show a rubric to your class before they begin the assignment.

Whether we use the simple Presentation Model with only a minor discussion or a highly interactive model, involving students lets us share the "burden of explanation" with them and we are no longer alone in explaining how to complete an assignment.

Avoiding student outrage is not, however, the main argument for involving students in rubric construction to some degree. Whether we use the simple Presentation Model, which involves only minor discussion, or the highly interactive 4×4 model, or something in between, by involving students, we share the "burden of explanation" with them and are no longer alone in explaining how to complete an assignment. Instead, we foster a discussion in which our students can tell us three basic things we need to know in order to make our explanation relevant:

- They tell us what they already know.
- They tell us what they don't know.
- They tell us what misconceptions and misunderstandings they have about the assignment.

By telling us what they know and don't know, students spare us considerable time and energy we might otherwise devote to unnecessary explanations and allow us to focus in on what really needs further explanation. In classes where student knowledge is highly uneven, students who are more advanced will also share what they know with their classmates who may not know it, thus sharing the teaching burden. This is desirable not only because students discussing ideas is a good thing, but because students are far more likely to retain knowledge that is not imparted by the professor (Light, 2001). They remember best the things they themselves said in class; second best, the things their classmates said; and last, the things the professors said. Thus, by sharing the "burden of explanation" through the rubric, we benefit both those students who understood something accurately, and who will now remember it all the better for having articulated their knowledge, and those who never knew it in the first place, who have now heard it in a form they are more likely to retain.

Each year the discussion of the first rubric presented in Portland State's Freshman Inquiry program is always an evaluation of the existing skills of the incoming class for the professor as well as a learning experience for the students.

For example, in one incoming class, the description of the highest expectation for the "Writing skills" dimension of the first rubric of the year, a three-level rubric with check boxes, generated markedly different responses within the same class, despite the fact that almost all the students were recent graduates of the same basic public school system. The description of the highest level of performance in the "Writing skills" dimension read:

- ❑ Spelling and grammar are accurate.
- ❑ Paragraphs are used appropriately and are internally well constructed.
- ❑ Transitions are smooth and logical.
- ❑ The tone is consistent and appropriate for a scholarly paper.

After presentation of the rubric, the student questions surfaced. Some were not even familiar with using a computer to assist with spelling and grammar. Others were unfamiliar with the concept of a Writing

Center or how to use one. The professor, who in this case had passed out information regarding the Writing Center and therefore considered his job done in that regard, was stunned to discover that several of his students thought this was a place where those who liked to write hung out, a form of campus club. And while he was explaining the nature and uses of the Writing Center, still other students in the same class were engaged in a lively discussion regarding the ideological reasons for using or not using "I" in an academic paper. Most of the class fell somewhere in between these extremes, and eventually these and many other questions were answered not by the professor, who wisely stuck to facilitating the process, but by the students themselves using the rubric as a mediator.

By creating a situation in which he invited his class to share what they did and did not know, this professor learned many things he needed to know about his students and the diverse nature of what turned out to be a lively but difficult class to teach. This is not unusual. He also learned that in many cases, his students did not really know what they thought they knew. The discussions that attend rubric construction are effective troubleshooting techniques for finding out the misconceptions and misunderstandings students may have without knowing it.

For example, in a Portland State interdisciplinary Sophomore Inquiry class on Asian Studies, the professor asked her students to write a paper analyzing three Web sites on Hindu deities with regard to how they did or did not reveal Orientalist assumptions. She considered this a simple assignment, especially since the three sites were specifically selected because they represented extreme Orientalist stereotypes about Asia. When she presented the grading rubric to her class, however, she was astonished to find that many of the students were puzzled that the "Analysis" dimension carried such weight. After some class discussion, it emerged that these students thought the assignment was to discuss Hindu deities using the three Web sites as authoritative for research purposes. What a good thing that the confusion was sorted out before the students devoted considerable effort to deliberately producing a poorly researched paper based entirely on questionable Internet sources!

Participation in rubric construction can also help to motivate students, partly because it helps them to understand the assignment better in its various parts, but also because this participation gives students a sense of ownership of the assignment. This is especially true when the participation is considerable. Lewis, Berghoff, and Pheeney (1999) studied the impact of "negotiated rubrics" on student motivation. Finding that negotiated rubrics create a greater sense of student involvement in the tasks assigned, they also noted that the papers produced showed a high level of professionalism and creativity.

Thus, collaborative construction of a rubric helps students understand assignment expectations; increases student motivation; and gives teachers invaluable feedback about their prior knowledge, skill levels, ability to self-assess, and motivation.

Five Models of Collaborative Rubric Construction

But how can you maintain control over your classroom and ensure that standards will be maintained while the foxes are not only guarding the henhouse, but often building it? The truth is that we never really give up that much control. Even when our students are racing about the classroom with Post-its or gathered in groups of four making lists to be presented in the 4×4 model—we retain the essential control over the structure and nature of the assignment. Beyond that is room for negotiation and student participation.

We control the process by which the rubric will be used in the classroom. We say whether the students' participation will be limited to discussion and questions as in the Presentation Model, expanded to include some input as in the pass-the-hat model, or extended as far as creating an entire rubric for our approval or disapproval as in the 4×4 model.

In Chapter 3, we described a four-stage process of rubric creation:

- *Stage 1: Reflecting* on the task and context
- *Stage 2: Listing* our learning objectives and expectations
- *Stage 3: Grouping and Labeling* the objective and criteria
- *Stage 4: Application* to a rubric grid format

Figure 4.1 shows how the stages can be used to understand the roles that professors and students play in our rubric construction models. As we move from Model 1, Presentation, to Model 5, 4×4, the professor plays a lesser role while the students play a larger role in rubric construction.

Rubric Construction Model	Stage 1: Reflecting	Stage 2: Listing	Stage 3: Grouping and Labeling	Stage 4: Application
1. Presentation	Professor	Professor	Professor	Professor and students who ask questions and reflect their own understandings
2. Feedback	Professor	Professor	Professor	Professor and students who edit for clarity
3. Pass-the-hat	Professor	Professor/ students	Professor and students who group student contributions	Professor and students who create final rubric
4. Post-it	Professor	Students	Professor and students who facilitate grouping	Professor and students who create final rubric
5. 4×4	Professor	Students	Students	Students

Figure 4.1 Professor and student rubric construction roles in models of rubric construction.

1. The Presentation Model

The Presentation Model is the most commonly used rubric construction model. In the Presentation Model, the teacher does all the work and makes all the major decisions. Following the stages set out in Chapter 3, you set the dimensions of the rubric by setting out what is expected in terms of fulfilling the specific assignment and presenting it in an acceptable, scholarly fashion. You also determine the weight that will be given to each dimension, decide on a scale and, pulling on past experience and current expectations, decide what constitutes an excellent fulfillment of the assignment, establish one or more acceptable levels of fulfillment, and describe the lowest level of performance (see Figure 4.2).

Rubric Construction Model	Stage 1: Reflecting	Stage 2: Listing	Stage 3: Grouping and Labeling	Stage 4: Application
1. Presentation	Professor	Professor	Professor	Professor and students who ask questions and reflect their own understandings

Figure 4.2 Professor and student rubric construction roles for the Presentation Model.

All that remains is to communicate the results of your labors to the students. You begin by passing out the rubric before your students have started the assignment for which the rubric will be used to grade and asking them to read it. That alone can be a challenge. We have found that some students tend to regard handouts as one more piece of information they don't have to write down and stow it away in their backpacks with only a cursory glance. Here again, we find that the obsession many students have with grades can be turned to our own advantage.

One way to ensure that they do read it and take it seriously is to ask them to staple the rubric to the completed assignment when they hand it in. No rubric, no grade, and maybe even a penalty besides. This not only saves paper and copying costs, but it also emphasizes the connection between the rubric and the grade.

That can be the end of it as far as the Presentation Model is concerned. However, we have found that we get better results from having the students do the preliminary reading of the rubric in class, followed by a call for questions. We usually allow some time not only for questions but also for some serious discussion of the criteria and expectations reflected in the rubric, but students really have no opportunity to revise the rubric. We may occasionally alter the rubric if something comes up in the discussion that needs clarification, but we neither make nor imply any promises beforehand.

Faced with a list of clear expectations, sometimes with actual grading points or percentages attached, many freshmen are motivated for the first time to ask such questions as:

- What's a citation, and what's an acceptable format for a citation?
- What do you mean by my own analysis of the work?
- Do we lose points if it is late?

We were often surprised by such questions, which reveal the students' lack of awareness about some of the most basic academic expectations. Explaining such details as what a footnote is, what MLA or APA formats are, when to use which, and the rest of whatever confusion the rubric presentation has caused can seem lengthy, but it's surely better than informing an entire class that no one got an A because no one cited sources or included a personal analysis or whatever the issue was. We know that, contrary to the rumors among some students, professors don't enjoy giving bad grades.

The Presentation Model, although not highly interactive, is an early warning system about student responses to and knowledge of expectations for professors and students alike. This model of rubric creation is well suited to large, lower-division, undergraduate classes in which lecturing is the main teaching style. The Presentation Model does not take up much class time. The professor does most of the talking and simply fields questions, which seldom takes more than half an hour and can take considerably less.

2. The Feedback Model

The Feedback Model differs from the Presentation Model only in that when we present the rubric to the class, it is with the understanding that it can still be changed through student feedback. Before the professor finalizes the rubric, the students are presented with a completed rubric but are given the option to revise it by making edits, offering ideas, and asking questions. Figure 4.3 summarizes the roles that professors and students play in constructing the rubric for the Feedback Model.

To foster student feedback, students can be divided into small groups to discuss the rubric and decide what needs clarification and elaboration. Suggestions then may be taken from a limited number of group spokespersons rather than from individuals. This not only cuts down on potential chaos, but also allows greater input from shy students and prevents the more verbal students from imposing their views on the others.

Rubric Construction Model	Stage 1: Reflecting	Stage 2: Listing	Stage 3: Grouping and Labeling	Stage 4: Application
2. Feedback	Professor	Professor	Professor	Professor and students who edit for clarity

Figure 4.3   Professor and student rubric construction roles for the Feedback Model.

In some cases, we encourage more active student participation by suggesting ways in which students might want to alter the rubric. One simple area in which to allow student input is in the weighting of the dimensions. Sometimes we include weighted dimensions that add up to only 70 percent of the final grade but allow students to decide both the weight and nature of the remaining 30 percent of the grading criteria. Sometimes we weight all dimensions equally and ask the students if they are comfortable with this strategy. Few are, and the discussions that follow can be very productive because students debate, often for the first time in their lives, the differing value of content, ideas, and the technical side of writing.

Another method is to leave parts of the rubric blank and ask students to fill it in. This works well with three- to five-level rubrics where we can fill in the best and worst expectations and ask the students to suggest what might lie midway between them. Not only does this force the students to read the dimension descriptions on each end carefully, but it also forces them to think back on their past experiences with academic writing including their past disasters. Students often add possibilities for disaster that we never even thought of. This method allows us to retain considerable control by including what we consider absolutely vital, while allowing the students considerable latitude in adding their input. Of course, we also take notes on their suggestions and eventually incorporate what we regard as valid into the final rubric.

In addition to the early warnings also provided by the Presentation Model, the Feedback Model can actually encourage quiet students to participate more fully. The promise of a better grade based on a rubric that at least partly highlights their strengths is a powerful incentive to speak up. Also, if we use the group presentations, the knowledge that their input will be presented as part of a group contribution and not an individual assertion often eases the way for students to understand that they do have something to contribute.

The need to contribute ideas also allows students to realize that assignments are not just hoops to leap through but a set of performance expectations that further their education in a variety of ways. Collaborating even in this initial way on the assessment tool itself indicates to students that they can self-assess against the rubric dimensions as they complete the assignment. Ideally, this will eventually lead them to self-assess with or without a rubric, thus becoming fully active learners.

The Feedback Model works best in smaller, lower-division undergraduate courses where discussion is part of the normal teaching style. In general, the Feedback Model is somewhat more time consuming than the Presentation Model because it encourages more active participation and discussion from the students. In general, however, it should not require more than one class period, and it can frequently be accomplished in less time.

3. The Pass-the-Hat Model

The Pass-the-Hat Model gives the students a maximum amount of flexibility and creativity in developing task expectations for a grading rubric, while allowing the professor to retain considerable control over the final product. In this model, the teacher does not create a rubric in advance but helps the students to create part of their own rubric during class time. Thus, students are involved in varying degrees in Stage 2 (Listing), Stage 3 (grouping and labeling), and Stage 4 (application). The students start with the professor-created assignment and list possible expectations for this assignment. The professor then groups and labels these expectations into dimensions and applies these to the rubric grid. Figure 4.4 summarizes these roles.

We begin by explaining both the assignment and the nature of a rubric as clearly as possible. Usually we try to use the Pass-the-Hat Model only with students who have already been introduced to the concept of rubrics through the Presentation or Feedback Models. In some cases, however, we have started students on a Pass-the-Hat Model of rubric construction without such previous experience. In those cases, we may pass out a generic rubric, usually a three-level

Rubric Construction Model	Stage 1: Reflecting	Stage 2: Listing	Stage 3: Grouping and Labeling	Stage 4: Application
3. Pass-the-Hat	Professor	Professor/ students	Professor and students who group student contributions	Professor and students who create final rubric

Figure 4.4   Professor and student rubric construction roles for the Pass-the-Hat Model.

rubric with the scales and possibly even some basic dimensions filled in to give students a better idea of what the finished product will look like. We also usually include a short presentation on rubrics, sometimes showing the students rubrics we have used in the past.

To begin the Pass-the-Hat exercise where we gather student input, we carefully review the assignment described in the syllabus. Then we pass out three to five slips of paper to each student and ask the students to write down what they think should define an A paper. We ask students to write only one suggestion per slip of paper. This facilitates Stage 3 (grouping and listing), allowing us to make the groupings for the rubric dimensions either in class or in our offices after class. We usually allow the students to consult with each other at this stage, and sometimes we actively organize them into groups.

We then collect the slips of paper in a hat or some other receptacle (some professors have great fun with this) and organize them into groups that will become the descriptions of the dimensions of the new rubric. Some professors prefer to take these slips to the privacy of their offices. However, doing the organization in front of the class creates greater student buy-in and also allows us to discuss the partly created rubric while student contributions and discussions are fresh in their own minds.

When we usually take their suggestions directly to our offices (mostly for time-related reasons) to do Stages 3 and 4, we are particularly careful to include student language in the final rubric as much as possible. This not only increases the legitimacy of the rubric in the students' eyes, but when we pass out the final version, at least one student is certain to announce proudly, "That's my bit." The others then start looking for their bits, and as a result the rubric gets carefully and thoroughly read.

Many professors who have never used the Pass-the-Hat Model worry about what to do if the students leave out a vitally important aspect of the assignment. The surprise for us has been that as a group they rarely do. If they do leave something out, however, we put it in. We may make the addition while we are collecting and organizing the slips of paper in front of the class. "No one mentioned citations," we announce looking shocked, and then we add it. Few students will forget to include citations in their papers after that.

Regardless of whether or not we read the contributions out loud and begin grouping them into dimensions in front of the class, the process always ends with us retiring to our offices to produce the finished rubric. Thereafter, the process takes on the form of the Presentation or Feedback Model, depending on whether or not further changes are permitted.

The Pass-the-Hat Model is well suited to small to medium-sized classes (fewer than thirty students) at any level where discussion is a regular part of the teaching method. Although highly interactive and learner centered, the Pass-the-Hat Model is not terribly time consuming, especially if the professor simply collects the student contributions and constructs the rubric outside of class. If the professor wishes to read off the student contributions, invite further comments, and suggest initial dimension categories, it will, of course, take considerably longer. In its simplest form, however, it seldom takes longer than half an hour.

4. The Post-it Model

An extension of the Pass-the-Hat Model, the Post-it Model gives greater control to the students who create not simply some of the descriptions of the dimensions, but the dimensions themselves. Figure 4.5 charts the roles that professors and students play. Students are more involved in Stages 2, 3, and 4 than in the previous models. Because the Post-it Model involves students in creating groups of ideas and creating dimensions, we give them Post-its rather than slips of paper to write their ideas on. Then they can stick their Post-its on the whiteboard, the walls, posters, or any other surface that seems useful and be able to move them around easily to create groups.

Rubric Construction Model	Stage 1: Reflecting	Stage 2: Listing	Stage 3: Grouping and Labeling	Stage 4: Application
4. Post-it	Professor	Students	Professor and students who facilitate grouping	Professor and students who create final rubric

Figure 4.5   Professor and student rubric construction roles for the Post-it Model.

We begin the Post-it Model in the same way we began the Pass-the-Hat Model. We pass out the Post-its and ask each student to write down two to three things he or she thinks should define an excellent fulfillment of the assignment, one per Post-it. We do not, however, collect these in a hat or any other receptacle. Instead, we invite the students to stick them on the whiteboard, blackboard, or any convenient wall.

Thereafter, chaos ensues. We ask the students to read one another's contributions and to try to organize them by putting related items together in the same area. We act as referees as they debate whether or not a Post-it reading "good ideas based on accurate facts" should be grouped with other Post-its dealing with ideas or with Post-its that relate to the importance of accurate research. What they are really doing, of course, is the grouping we would otherwise do in the Pass-the-Hat Model to create the dimensions of the new rubric. "Good ideas based on accurate facts" actually belongs in at least two dimensions (to be labeled "Analysis" and "Content," perhaps) and really should have been written on two separate Post-its, but we let the students figure that out. In general, there are enough other Post-its bearing similar suggestions that this one need not be torn in half or duplicated, although that does sometimes occur. One major revelation students often mention after participating in the Post-it Model is a greater awareness of how the elements of good writing overlap and interact with each other.

Once the student contributions are grouped, we bring in poster boards or, if we can get them, the largest Post-it boards. We stick or prop these up around the classroom and call for volunteers; each volunteer is given a black marker and a poster or large Post-it. Then we read off all the contributions in a single group and ask the class to come up with a title for the dimension that binds these together. Usually we demand they come up with a single word, although we've been known to settle for two or even three word titles; we've also been known to do some prompting at this stage. Once the class decides on a dimension title, a volunteer writes it on the top of one of the posters and copies the main descriptions from the original grouped Post-its onto the final poster. At this stage, it is not unusual for students to spot an omission and add new descriptions to the final list.

We then move on to the next loose grouping of Post-its and repeat the process. Once all the posters are completed, we collect them, take them back to our offices, and create the final rubric.

The Post-it Model is best suited to smaller, upper-division or graduate courses where students already have a fairly strong academic background. In larger classes, it is apt to cause confusion, partly because students are not accustomed to designing their own grading tool and partly because academic discipline is likely to be looser. In addition, the room design itself, with bolted-down seats filled to the side walls, may not foster collaboration.

The Post-it Model is quite time consuming and is mostly intended for large, complex, and end-of-term assignments. It can take as many as two or even three class periods. The time is seldom wasted, however. Even with upper division and graduate students, misconceptions can and do occur, and the extended discussions that accompany the grouping and labeling brings out these misconceptions.

5. The 4×4 Model

Anderson's (1998) 4×4 Model has some elements of control but allows for student input at all stages of the rubric construction process. In this model, the professor's role is limited to setting the assignment, explaining what the finished rubric will look like in a generic sense, and facilitating the creation of the rubric by the students. The students fully participate in all stages of creating the final rubric, as indicated in the summary chart in Figure 4.6.

To begin the process, we refer to the syllabus and read the assignment description. We then divide the students into groups of four; at

Rubric Construction Model	Stage 1: Reflecting	Stage 2: Listing	Stage 3: Grouping and Labeling	Stage 4: Application
5. 4×4	Professor/ students	Students	Students	Students

Figure 4.6 Professor and student rubric construction roles for the 4×4 Model.

least, four is the number used by Anderson (1998), but we have found that it's not essential to be that exact. In these groups, students draw on their own experiences to identify and discuss four task dimensions that they think are most important in successfully completing the assignment for which the rubric is to be designed. Each group writes down its list of four task dimensions on a board, an overhead transparency, or even a PowerPoint slide if computer projection technology is available.

One spokesperson from each group then presents the group's work to the class, focusing on one task dimension out of the four, possibly the one that generated the most discussion or about which everyone felt the most passion. As facilitators, we help identify similarities and differences among the various groups' task dimensions, but we avoid taking sides. After each group has presented its task dimensions, we ask the entire class to vote on which top four should be included in the rubric. Some professors insist on a consensus; we usually settle for a two-thirds majority vote. This is not always easy to achieve, and the groups may have to meet and develop a second or even a third set of task dimensions before finding four they can all (or two-thirds of them, anyway) agree on. The four task dimensions selected by this method become the dimensions of the new rubric.

The students return to their groups and write four descriptions for each of the task dimensions describing four levels of performance from 1 to 4, with 4 being the highest and 1 being the lowest. These descriptions are again shared with the class using a board, an over-head, or a computer projection. As before, we act as facilitators, pointing out similarities and contrasts in each group's efforts. Finally, the class discusses the descriptions and votes on the results until con-sensus or a two-thirds majority is reached. The results then become the descriptions of the dimensions on the new rubric.

Sometimes we send the students back to their groups at this point to label the scale of the new rubric with something more descriptive than four numbers. We try to provide encouraging, nonjudgmental labels like "Exemplary," "Proficient," "Developing," and "Emerging," but ultimately this too is a student decision.

The 4×4 Model is almost entirely a student creation. We simply take what has been produced in class and put it in a tidier form. We may sometimes tweak a few points, but students should recognize their work in the rubric.

The 4×4 Model is suitable to any level and almost any size class (more than eight and fewer than one hundred students). Despite the high level of student involvement, it works well even with freshmen because of the ample opportunity it affords for group reflection and refinement of initial ideas; if teaching assistants are available to circulate and monitor groups, so much the better. Freshmen are often surprised to discover that they know a lot more about what constitutes good academic work than they ever imagined.

Because the 4×4 Model takes even more time than the Post-it Model, often as much as one to two full class periods, it is best suited to large, content-heavy assignments such as research papers or term projects. You and your students will quickly discover that rubric dimensions and the descriptions of those dimensions cannot be developed in any meaningful way without also discussing the assignment and the content of the class. Thus, the time allocated for rubric creation can be blended with the time allocated for class discussions of content.

Conclusion

In this chapter we have described how we integrate rubrics and rubric construction into our teaching methods. We have also offered some advice, based on our own experiences, on how to determine which approach is best for different levels and class sizes and for different types of assignments. But don't take our word for it. Experiment for yourself. You can also combine different aspects of these five models to create your own model for your own unique teaching style and your own unique classes.

5

RUBRIC CONSTRUCTION WITH OTHERS: TEACHING ASSISTANTS, TUTORS, OR COLLEAGUES

How many professors does it take to construct a rubric? The same number it takes to change a lightbulb: one, plus maybe a few students. For a long time, those seemed to be the two options. We constructed our rubrics in the privacy of our offices and presented them to our classes (Presentation Model; see Chapter 4), and that was the beginning of clear communication of our expectations to students. At other times, we involved our students in rubric construction, using one of the models of rubric construction described in Chapter 4. Recently, however, we have found that involving our teaching assistants, the Writing Center, other tutorial staff, and even our colleagues in the act of rubric construction can often make our rubrics more effective as assessment and teaching tools as well as time-saving grading devices.

Involving Teaching Assistants in Rubric Construction

Certainly we have good reasons to involve our T.A.s in rubric construction. T.A.s are, by their very nature, there to help us, something they can do much better if they understand what we are trying to accomplish. Virtually all T.A.s appreciate a certain amount of leadership; they are inexperienced as instructors or graders and are often apprehensive. Even T.A.s who will not be grading have much to gain from being involved in rubric construction. Rubric construction requires articulating what is and is not important for each assignment and for the class overall. Simply knowing that can help a T.A. become better at leading discussion sections, overseeing labs, running practice sessions, or doing whatever it is T.A.s assist with in different disciplines. Also, because many T.A.s plan to become professors eventually, involving them in rubric construction models good teaching practice.

T.A.s can also help us with rubrics regardless of whether or not they will be using them to grade. They are, as a rule, closer to the students and can often offer insights into what needs to be spelled out and what does not.

Collaborating with T.A.s who are going to be doing some or all of our grading is routine. We don't simply hand a stack of papers to a T.A. without offering some guidelines about how they are to be graded. Many professors who have never heard of a grading rubric regularly hand their T.A.s lists of key points they want to see covered in the papers; these lists are, in fact, the same kinds of lists we produced as part of the Stage 2 (listing) or Stage 3 (grouping and labeling) discussed in Chapter 3. As with so much of rubric construction, creating a rubric with a T.A. is simply a more systematized version of something most of us do anyway.

The key question we must ask ourselves is how much control over rubric creation we want to give to the T.A. The more work we do ourselves, the less opportunity the T.A. has for input and the less the T.A. is able to assist us. As noted earlier, even professors who do not care to have their T.A.s do anything beyond leading discussion, lab, or practice sections, and who prefer to do their own grading, still have something to gain from at least consulting T.A.s on rubric construction. For other professors, there is an escalating possibility for T.A. involvement to be considered:

- Professor creates the rubric and gives it to the T.A. to use in grading.

- Professor creates a list of the basic dimensions and main points (Stage 3, grouping and labeling, as shown in Chapter 3) but lets the T.A. create the rubric; the professor checks the rubric and makes changes before allowing it to be used for grading.

- Professor creates a list of goals and key points (Stage 2, listing, as shown in Chapter 3) and lets the T.A. create a rubric; the professor checks the rubric and makes changes before allowing it to be used for grading.

- Professor tells the T.A. to create a rubric but checks it and makes changes before it is used for grading.

Working with a T.A. can also be combined with working with the students. Often T.A.-led discussion sections are far more suitable places for the more time-consuming forms of interactive rubric construction such as the Post-it, Pass-the-Hat, or 4×4 Models described in Chapter 4. We often find it useful to have the T.A. work with the students to produce a rubric. However, we never give up the right to look over, veto, or make changes in a rubric created entirely by students and a T.A.

Involving Tutorial Staff in Rubric Construction

Collaborating on a rubric with a T.A. is usually just a more explicit way of delegating tasks and sharing our expectations. Collaborating directly with staff from the Writing Center, math tutors, librarians, computer specialists, or other academic facilities designed to provide specific forms of assistance to our students, however, is something else. Some professors do this when they assign a major paper or project in a class where they know many of the students lack the necessary skills.

For example, professors in Portland State University's Freshman Inquiry sometimes collaborate with the Writing Center on the grading rubric for a research paper that is a required component of the second term of the yearlong class. They know that many students still have serious writing problems at this stage, and the Writing Center staff will inevitably be involved one way or another. Collaborating with them on rubric construction allows them to give useful input and ask questions that will inevitably come up anyway.

Even when we do not collaborate directly with supporting student services, however, a rubric means that we collaborate with them indirectly through the rubric. We always notify support services about our use of rubrics and suggest that they insist on seeing the rubric whenever they are helping one of our students. When working closely with student services on complex and important assignments, this kind of collaboration takes no more than a few minutes on the phone. An e-mail message with the rubric attached is equally easy and useful.

For the most part, these notifications are met with gratitude. Rubrics provide a much richer array of information about the assignment than most students can generally offer, and most support staff find them a great aid in figuring out how to guide students in completing their assignments.

Involving Colleagues in Rubric Construction

Collaborating with colleagues on grading rubrics is a far less common occurrence. In general, it occurs only when we are team teaching or mentoring junior faculty or adjuncts. In both cases, however, collaborating on grading rubrics can be a rewarding experience for faculty, because it offers them an opportunity to discuss shared goals and teaching methodologies and also a chance to evaluate and validate their own grading practices.

Rubrics are certainly useful in providing needed consistency in team-taught classes. The term *team teaching* is usually applied to classes in which two or more professors teach a single class, but it can also apply to classes that are supposed to be the same, but are taught by different professors (e.g., 17 sections of first-year French language or 22 sections of Introduction to American Studies).

Sharing rubrics for major assignments in cases like these provides some consistency, without taking away from the flexibility and personalized approach most professors correctly expect to have in their classrooms. Sharing rubrics with colleagues can also reveal whether or not grading is more or less consistent.

Professors at Portland State, in a Freshman Inquiry class titled "Metamorphosis," created a rubric together. Although described as "team taught," in fact the professors differed considerably in their approaches, assignments, and even texts. This was not too surprising. The seven professors involved in teaching the class included two English professors, one historian, one gender studies scholar, a chemist, and a political scientist. To add chaos to confusion, two members of the team did not teach at Portland State but at a community college. All members of this team subscribed to the same general thematic organization and met regularly to exchange information on what was going on in the various classes. They shared one text per quarter and one assignment per year—a research paper on "a person, institution, or movement that has created or sought to create significant change." Each professor was welcome to add his or her own requirements and limitations to that very broad assignment.

When the Metamorphosis team decided to put its research paper assignment to the test with a shared rubric that all team members would use to grade their students' papers, regardless of how the assignment had been altered for each class, they anticipated major problems. To begin with, they knew they had different teaching styles and opinions; they often clashed, albeit amicably, in their team meetings. Some gave their students extremely specific directions and limited the kinds of persons, institutions, or movements their students could choose. Others left the field wide open.

Yet when they sat down to begin Stage 2 of rubric construction, listing (see Chapter 3), they discovered that they differed far less than expected—to paraphrase Gertrude Stein, "a research paper is a research paper is a research paper." Their lists were remarkably similar and, with a little help from a consultant (who gently explained about grids, dimensions, and the other aspects of rubric design discussed in this book), they produced a rubric that was acceptable to all of them. The final collaboratively constructed rubric is shown in Figure 5.1.

The only real point of contention was that some of the professors wanted to ascribe different points to different dimensions. They resolved this problem by assigning no points to any dimension; professors were free to add them or to leave the matter of points to their own discretion. Given such flexibility, the Metamorphosis team expected that the rubric would reveal inconsistent grading practices. However, when a group of outside graders were brought in to provide a second opinion, the results showed that not only was grading very consistent across the team, but by using the rubric, nonteam members were also able to grade consistently and fairly (Redder, 2003).

This last advantage is of particular importance when we consider one other group of colleagues with whom we might want to share rubrics: adjuncts. The increasing use of adjuncts rather than new tenure track professors is regrettable but real. Rubrics will not solve the many overall problems this practice causes, but it can address the immediate issue of integrating an adjunct into an existing department and set of classes as rapidly as possible. Most professors and

Grading Rubric for Metamorphosis Paper

Task Description: Write a research paper about a person, institution, or movement that has created or sought to create significant change. (Professors were allowed to add to this description but not to subtract from it.)

High mastery	Average mastery	Low mastery
Communication		
□ An inviting introduction draws the reader in, a satisfying conclusion leaves the reader with a sense of closure and resolution.	□ The paper has a recognizable introduction and conclusion, but the introduction may not create a strong sense of anticipation or the conclusion may not tie the paper into a coherent whole.	□ There is no real lead-in to set up what follows and no real conclusion to wrap things up.
□ *There is a clear thesis.*	□ *There is a thesis but it is ambiguous or unfocused.*	□ *There is no clear thesis.*
□ Transitions are thoughtful and clearly show how ideas connect.	□ Transitions often work well, but some leave connections between ideas fuzzy.	□ Connections between ideas are often confusing or missing.
□ *Uses an appropriate variety of sources, which are well integrated and support the author's points.*	□ *Sources generally support the author's points, but more or a greater variety need to be cited.*	□ *Citations are infrequent or often seem to fail to support the author's points.*
□ Quotations, paraphrases, and summaries are used and cited appropriately.	□ Quotations, paraphrases, and summaries generally work but occasionally interfere with the flow of the writing, seem irrelevant, or are incorrectly cited.	□ Quotations, paraphrases, and summaries tend to break the flow of the piece, become monotonous, don't seem to fit, or are not cited.
□ *Uses the proper format (APA, MLA, etc.)*	□ Uses the proper format but there are occasional errors.	□ *Frequent errors in format or incorrect format used.*
□ Sequencing is logical and effective.	□ Sequencing shows some logic, but it is not under complete control and may be so predictable than the reader finds it distracting.	□ Sequencing seems illogical, disjointed, or forced.
□ Spelling is generally correct even on more difficult words.	□ *Spelling is generally correct, but more difficult words may be misspelled.*	□ *There are frequent spelling errors, even on common words.*
□ Punctuation is accurate, even creative, and guides the reader effectively through the text.	□ End punctuation is correct, but internal punctuation is sometimes missing or wrong.	□ Punctuation is often missing or incorrect, including terminal punctuation.
□ *Grammar and usage contribute to the clarity; conventions, if manipulated for stylistic effect, work.*	□ *There are problems with grammar or usage, but they are not serious enough to distort meaning.*	□ *Errors in grammar or usage are frequent enough to become distracting and interfere with meaning.*
□ Voice and style are appropriate for the type of paper assigned.	□ Voice and style don't quite fit with the type of paper assigned.	□ Voice and style are not appropriate for the type of paper assigned.
□ *Paragraphs are well-focused and coherent.*	□ *Paragraphs occasionally lack focus or coherence.*	□ *Paragraphs generally lack focus or coherence.*

Critical Thinking

☐ The paper displays insight and originality of thought.	☐ There are some original ideas, but many seem obvious or elementary.	☐ There are few original ideas; most seem obvious or elementary.
☐ *There is sound and logical analysis that reveals clear understanding of the relevant issues.*	☐ *Analysis is generally sound, but there are lapses in logic or understanding.*	☐ *Analysis is superficial or illogical, the author seems to struggle to understand the relevant issues.*
☐ There is an appropriate balance of factual reporting, interpretation and analysis, and personal opinion.	☐ The balance between factual reporting, interpretation and analysis, and personal opinion seems skewed.	☐ There is a clear imbalance among factual reporting, interpretation and analysis, and personal opinion.
☐ *The author goes beyond the obvious in constructing interpretation of the facts.*	☐ *Paper shows understanding of relevant issues but lacks depth.*	☐ *Author appears to misunderstand or omit key issues.*
☐ Telling and accurate details are used to reinforce the author's arguments.	☐ Generally accurate details are included but the reader is left with questions—more information is needed to fill in the blanks.	☐ There are few details or most details seem irrelevant.
☐ *The paper is convincing and satisfying.*	☐ *The paper leaves the reader vaguely skeptical and unsatisfied.*	☐ *The paper leaves the reader unconvinced.*

Content

☐ The paper addresses a topic within the context of promoting personal, social/cultural/political, or paradigmatic change.	☐ The paper addresses a topic within the context of promoting personal, social/cultural/political, or paradigmatic change.	☐ The paper needs to be substantially more closely related to promoting personal, social/cultural/political, or paradigmatic change.
☐ *The paper is complete and leaves no important aspect of the topic not addressed.*	☐ *The paper is substantially complete, but more than one important aspect of the topic is not addressed.*	☐ *The paper is clearly incomplete with many important aspects of the topic left out.*
☐ The author has a good grasp of what is known, what is generally accepted, and what is yet to be discovered.	☐ The author has a good grasp of the relevant information but fails to distinguish among what is known, what is generally accepted, and what is yet to be discovered.	☐ The author has a poor grasp of the relevant information.
☐ *Appropriate significance is assigned to the information presented and irrelevant information is rarely included.*	☐ *The paper often used information in a way inappropriate to its significance or includes much irrelevant information.*	☐ *The paper frequently uses information inappropriately or uses irrelevant information.*
☐ Connections between the topic of the paper and related topics are made that enhance understanding.	☐ Few connections are made to related topics.	☐ No connections are made to related topics to help clarify the information presented.
☐ *Specialized terminology, if used, is used correctly and precisely.*	☐ *Specialized terminology is sometimes incorrectly or imprecisely used.*	☐ *Specialized terminology is frequently misused.*
☐ The author seems to be writing from personal knowledge or experience.	☐ The author seems to be writing from knowledge or experience but has difficulty going from general observations to specifics.	☐ The work seems to be a simple restatement of the assignment or a simple, overly broad answer to a question with little evidence of expertise on the part of the author.

Figure 5.1 *Continued*

department chairs routinely share syllabi previously used for the classes the incoming adjunct will teach. This is partly to help the adjunct write a new syllabus quickly by borrowing ideas, but it is also a way of telling the newcomer what the department expects her or him to cover in the course.

Looking over a selection of previous professors' syllabi can provide an adjunct with ideas for organization, texts, and assignments, so a selection of rubrics can give the newcomer a whole array of ideas regarding what to expect from the students in terms of their work. Adjuncts who receive rubrics when they begin a new teaching position often begin using and even constructing rubrics themselves, thus leaving their own records for the department and creating a record of their own teaching successes that can form a valuable part of their employment prospectuses as they search for tenure track jobs.

Rubrics can also serve this purpose for any professor who is not yet tenured or who is seeking promotion. A selection of rubrics not only shows what was assigned but leaves an easy-to-read record of the professor's expectations and how well the students she or he taught were ultimately able to meet those expectations.

Conclusion

This chapter explored the many benefits of collaborating on rubric construction and use with others. Even though it takes extra time, there are some real advantages to involving others in the construction of rubrics. This is true of T.A.s, librarians, and other support staff whose job is to help our students meet our expectations. Rubrics can also provide departments with a better record of shared expectations, continuity, and academic standards, and they provide individual faculty members with evidence of their own teaching skills. Above all, sharing rubric construction with others gives us, in the long run, more input about how we communicate our expectations.

6

GRADING WITH RUBRICS

Rubrics do many things in terms of student learning, classroom communication, and even collegial collaboration, but when the clock starts nudging its way toward the wee hours of the morning, the ways in which rubrics make grading faster and easier is when their value becomes obvious. Rubrics make grading easier and faster in several ways:

- Establishing performance anchors
- Providing detailed, formative feedback (three- to five-level rubrics)
- Supporting individualized, flexible, formative feedback (scoring guide rubrics)
- Conveying summative feedback (grade)

These four ways are generally chronological in nature. Establishing performance anchors helps us get started more quickly and also more fairly. Three- to five-level rubrics allow us to provide detailed, formative feedback very rapidly by simply checking and circling prewritten criteria, whereas scoring guide rubrics allow us to do the same thing more flexibly and in a more individualized fashion, albeit at the cost of speed. Finally, by conveying summative feedback in an easy to read, almost graphic fashion, rubrics enable us to assign grades more rapidly and defend them more easily.

Indeed, many of us find the speedy, graphic nature of grading with rubrics so appealing that we have begun to use them to grade ourselves. In this chapter, we will also include examples of such grading with "metarubrics." Metarubrics are rubrics we have developed over the years to grade our own courses, to evaluate how effective our texts, lectures, and other teaching strategies really are. We even have a metarubric to evaluate our rubrics.

Most of us do this mentally as we grade, noting the results of our teaching in our students' work. Some of us even remember to write down our thoughts if we have the time. But using simple metarubrics speeds the process of instructional self-assessment to the point where time is not much of an issue, and we really can take notes as we grade of what works and what doesn't, thus providing ourselves with a rich source of information to improve our teaching, texts, and rubrics the next time we teach that particular course, even if the next time is a year or more later (see Chapter 10).

Performance Anchors: Being Consistent and Focused

There they sit: a pile of papers awaiting our attention. We all have our tricks. We divide them up into batches of ten, batches of five if it's a particularly long assignment. As we finish each batch, we reward ourselves. One of our colleagues places little wrapped candy mints (a great favorite of hers) in the pile every five papers, not to be eaten until they are uncovered. Another plows right in, refusing to count how many there are, refusing even to snack until he's finished. Silly little tricks, but useful and innocent.

Any kind of rubric, or scoring guide rubric, can eliminate such little tricks. With rubrics, we grade faster than without rubrics. With rubrics, we know what we want from the very beginning when we tell the students about the assignment. We often find that we grade the earlier papers on the stack at roughly the same speed as later papers. We may find that sometimes we can even pick up speed as we go along as we note how this particular class responded to the assignment. With rubrics, we focus our attention on what we expect in the best and worst papers, and we do it the same way—in the same order—for each and every paper.

Detailed, Formative Feedback: Gaining Speed

We'll also notice an increase in speed because we are no longer writing extensive notes on the back of each and every paper. No more writing "good ideas, but you need to work on developing them more fully" 30 times on as many papers. Just a few quick checks or circles on the rubric, or a word or two on a scoring guide rubric, and it's done. Our notes on the paper itself will probably be limited to proofreading and perhaps an occasional "good" or "check reference." If we feel we must add an individualized note, and many of us do, we can do that too.

Checks, circles, and a few well-chosen words are the keys to how rubrics speed up our grading process and make it easier while still giving detailed, formative feedback. Which of these we use depends on whether we are using

- Three- to five-level rubrics with check boxes (checks)
- Three- to five-level rubrics with circled text (circles)
- Scoring guide rubrics for narrative feedback (words)

In general, the degree to which rubrics facilitate grading by avoiding repetition is in direct inverse ratio to how long it took us to create the rubric. Some rubrics take longer to construct precisely because we are adding all of those feedback details ahead of time— that is, before the students even start the assignment.

Three- to five-level rubrics with check boxes are the most time consuming to create but the fastest and easiest to use. Three- to five-level rubrics that require us to circle relevant text take a bit more time to use. Scoring guide rubrics designed to give narrative feedback are the easiest and fastest to create, but their grading ease is somewhat limited by the time it takes to write out the feedback.

The three- to five-level rubric with check boxes is easily the most refined grading tool and also the fastest to use. It is especially appropriate for grading something that requires detailed feedback and particular speed such as an oral presentation. We simply check off categories as we go, possibly circling parts of the description here and there to further refine the details of what caused our positive or negative response. Note in the three- to five-level rubric in Figure 6.1 how the professor was able to tell a student that his speaking voice was generally good but that he spoke too fast, that his PowerPoints were too verbose, and that his conclusions were too implicit. All this accomplished with a few quick checks and circles.

The three- to five-level rubric with circled text takes a bit more time and thought to use effectively and is best suited to written assignments, although it can be used for oral presentations and other fast-moving grading moments if handled correctly. In using a three- to five-level

Rubric for Film Presentation

Task Description: Working in groups of four or five, students will develop and present to the class an analysis of a Japanese movie about World War II. This analysis should go beyond a simple synopsis of the movie to discuss how well or poorly the film reflects a particular point of view about the war. You are expected to do additional research to develop this presentation and to use visual aids of some sort. All groups members are expected to participate in the presentation.

	Exemplary	Competent	Developing
Individual presentation skills	☐ The presenter spoke clearly, slowly, and loudly enough to be heard without shouting, and modulated voice tone and quality. ☑ The presenter used expressive, appropriate body language and maintained eye contact with the audience. ☐ The presenter used all the time allotted but did not speak too long. ☑ The presenter used humor and anecdotes appropriately to liven up and illustrate the presentation. ☑ The presenter or an assistant competently handled the equipment.	☑ The presenter was understood but mumbled, spoke (too fast) or too slow, whispered, shouted, or droned: intelligibility however, was not compromised. ☐ The presenter's body language did not distract significantly, but the presenter fidgeted, remained rigid, never looked at the audience, or engaged in other inappropriate body language. ☑ The presenter's timing was (too long) or too brief. ☐ Humor and anecdotes were used, but they were over- or underused to liven up and or illustrate the presentation. ☐ Equipment was used, but there was some fumbling although not to the point where it seriously distracted from the presentation.	☐ The presenter mumbled, spoke too fast or too slow, whispered or shouted, or droned to the point where intelligibility was compromised. ☐ The presenter fidgeted, remained rigid, never looked at the audience, or engaged in other body language that distracted seriously from the content. ☐ The presenter barely used the time allotted or used much too much time. ☐ The lack of humor and anecdotes made the presentation dull. ☐ There was a lot of fumbling with the equipment that could have been prevented with a little practice.
Group presentation skills	☑ The presentation allowed each member an equal opportunity to shine. ☐ The individual presentations followed one another in a way that promoted a logical discussion of the topic, and connections between individual presentations were clearly shown. ☑ Members treated each other with courtesy and respect.	☐ The presentation was unbalanced in the way time or content was assigned to members. ☑ The individual presentations followed one another in a way that mostly promoted a logical discussion of the topic, but connections between individual presentations were not clearly shown, or the presentation lost direction from time to time for other reasons. ☐ Group members mostly treated each other with courtesy and respect, but there were lapses where members were not listening to each other.	☐ The presentation was seriously unbalanced so that one or a few people dominated or carried the ball. ☐ There was little if any evident logic in how the individual presentations followed one another, and the connections between individual presentations were unclear. ☐ Group members showed little respect or courtesy toward one another.

Figure 6.1 Three-level rubric with check boxes. Note how the professor has used checks and circles to clarify and individualize feedback.

	Exemplary	Competent	Developing
Group organization	☐ The group thesis is clearly stated at the beginning and carried through in the rest of the presentation. ☐ The topics to be covered are introduced and the direction the overall presentation will take is made clear.	☐ The group thesis emerges from the presentation but is either unclear, unstated, or not stated directly. ☐ A clear thesis is stated, but it is not carried through in the presentation. ☑ Topics to be covered and the direction the presentation will take are stated, but they are not the topics covered or the direction actually taken.	☐ There is no stated group thesis. ☐ There is no indication of what topics will be covered or what direction that coverage will take. ☐ No order or focus emerges in the course of the presentation.
Individual organization	☑ The individual presentation was well organized in itself with an introduction, body, and conclusion. ☐ That organization was emphasized and made clear to the audience through the use of appropriately captioned PowerPoints, overheads, or handouts.	☐ The individual presentation was mostly well organized, but there were problems with the introduction, body, or conclusion. ☑ The presenter used PowerPoints, overheads, or handouts, but these were too wordy or too vague to help the audience follow the organization.	☐ The presentation rambled with little evidence of the introduction, body, or conclusion. ☐ PowerPoints, overheads, or handouts either were not used or did not assist the audience in following the organization in any significant way.
Individual content	☑ Facts and examples were detailed, accurate, and appropriate. ☑ Theories referenced were accurately described and appropriately used. ☐ Analyses, discussions, and conclusions were explicitly linked to examples, facts, and theories.	☐ Facts and examples were mostly detailed, accurate, and appropriate, but there were lapses. ☐ Theories referenced but they were either not accurately described or not appropriately used. ☑ The connection among analyses, discussions, and conclusions is evident or implied, but it is not explicitly linked to examples, facts, and theories.	☐ Facts and examples were seriously lacking in detail, inaccurate, or inappropriate. ☐ Theories referenced were inaccurately described and inappropriately used or not referenced or used at all. ☐ There is no clear connection among analyses, discussions, and examples, facts, and theories.

Figure 6.1 *Continued*

rubric without check boxes, we simply circle those parts of the rubric that apply; usually this means circling those whole descriptions that apply to a specific part of the assignment. In some cases, however, depending on how we wrote the dimension descriptions, it may mean circling bits of two or more descriptions in the same dimension to indicate a mixed response. Either way, without the check boxes breaking the descriptions down into even more detailed categories, this kind of rubric requires us to read more of the rubric as we work. And that, in turn, takes more time.

How much more time? Not a lot, really. We find that the absence of check boxes slows us down for the first few assignments we grade, but after that, we become played into the options and where they appear on the rubric and circle almost as speedily as we could check. The results, however, are often untidy and harder for the student to read. Figure 6.2 aptly illustrates the use of the three- to five-level rubric with circled text as feedback. It is the same rubric as the one with check boxes only more simply written, with circling substituted for the individual checked-off boxes.

In its finished form, this rubric proved not only more difficult to use in the short time allotted to the student presentation, but it was also harder for the students to understand. It was also just plain sloppy to look at. The reason for this was its complexity. The professor was equally interested in the content and the method of presentation. With less complex rubrics, circling works very well, as can be seen in Figure 6.3. This is an all-purpose "presentation rubric" for business students.

Because the criteria the professor is evaluating are fairly simple, circling works well. In only one case, "Elocution," is any further clarification needed to show that the problem was one of speaking too softly rather than too rapidly. The use of letter grades with pluses or minuses allows for some fine tuning; the B+ for content, for example, tells the student that, although not quite professional, the content was generally well handled, whereas the B− in eye contact suggests that this is an area that still needs some work.

Individualized, Flexible Feedback: A Trade-Off

Three- to five-level rubrics, checked or circled, save an enormous amount of time when grading and provide incredibly rich feedback.

Why, then, would anyone care to use the more time-consuming scoring guide rubric to grade student work?

One easy reason is that although the actual grading process takes longer with a scoring guide rubric, creating the guide itself is less time-consuming. This is not an equal trade-off, however. In the long run, scoring guide rubrics save less time than three- to five-level rubrics.

Scoring guide rubrics do, however, have two other advantages. They allow for much greater individualization and flexibility in grading. This makes them the grading tool of choice in cases where we want to allow our students as much freedom as possible. Scoring guide rubrics are therefore usually reserved for graduate students and creative assignments.

And scoring guide rubrics do save time in grading, just not as much time as three- to five-level rubrics do. They are essentially a format for the notes we would otherwise write freehand on a piece of student work, but that format is the all-important part when it comes to grading. That format supplies the focus that speeds up grading even in cases where we still write as many notes as before, sometimes more. That format also provides a structure to our notes so that we don't have to worry about what to say first and how the various elements relate to one another. The scoring guide rubric essentially organizes our notes for us.

It can also save considerable time in making notes, provided that we are grading a strong work. Since the criteria of the scoring guide rubric spell out the highest level of performance, often our notes are limited to noting that the student has met these standards or perhaps almost met them. In some cases, we may find pleasure in taking the time to add some further explication of how the student has exceeded our demands or expectations. That's always time well spent, even at 3 o'clock in the morning.

Figure 6.4 illustrates a completed rubric for a very good film presentation in a graduate seminar on World War II in film. The professor literally produced these notes and the grade (an A) as the student spoke; the professor's written comments are shown in script.

Note how the professor's notes for the "Introduction," "Organization," and "Presentation" sections merely commented briefly on how well the student had fulfilled the highest expectations for these sections, whereas the notes for "Context" and "Evidence" itemized

Rubric for Film Presentation

Task Description: Working in groups of four or five, students will develop and present to the class an analysis of a Japanese movie about World War II. This analysis should go beyond a simple synopsis of the movie to discuss how well or poorly the film reflects a particular point of view about the war. You are expected to do additional research to develop this presentation and to use visual aids of some sort. All group members are expected to participate in the presentation.

	Exemplary	Competent	Developing
Individual presentation skills 20%	The presenter spoke clearly and intelligibly, modulating voice tone and quality, maintaining eye contact, and using appropriate body language. The use of humor and competent handling of technology also contributed to the excellence of the presentation. The presenter used all the time available but did not go over the time limit.	The presenter was intelligible but mumbled or droned, spoke too fast or too slow, whispered or shouted, used inappropriate body language, inappropriate excessive, or too little humor or technical problems detracted from the presentation. The presentation ran over or under the time limit but not dramatically.	The presenter mumbled or droned, spoke too fast or too slow, whispered or shouted, used inappropriate body language, or failed to maintain eye contact to the point where intelligibility was compromised. Too much or too little humor or technological problems seriously detracted from the presentation. The presentation ran seriously over or under the time limit.
Group presentation skills 20%	The presentations followed a logical progression and allowed each member an equal opportunity to shine. Group members treated each other with courtesy and respect and assisted each other as needed.	The presentations followed a logical progression but were unbalanced in the way time or content was assigned to members, or the division of labor was fair but impeded the logical progression of the argument. Group members were mostly respectful and helpful toward one another, but there were lapses.	The presentations followed no logical progression, seriously overlapped one another, or allowed one or a few people to dominate. Group members showed little respect or courtesy toward one another and did not assist one another even when it was clear that a group member was in trouble.
Group organization 20%	The group thesis, topics to be covered and the direction the individual presentations will like are clearly stated at the beginning and carried through in the rest of the presentation.	The thesis, topics to be covered, and the direction the individual presentations will take are clearly stated at the beginning but not carried through in the rest of the presentation, or the thesis, topics to be covered, and direction emerge in the presentation but are not clearly stated in the introduction.	The thesis, topics, and direction are unclear, unstated, or not evident in the body of the presentation.

Figure 6.2   Three-level rubric with circled feedback.

	Exemplary	Competent	Developing
Individual organization 20%	The individual presentation was well organized in itself with an introduction, body, and conclusion. That organization was emphasized and made clear to the audience through the use of appropriately captioned PowerPoints, overheads, or handouts.	The individual presentation was mostly well organized but there were problems with the introduction, body, or conclusion. The presenter used PowerPoints, overheads, or handouts, but these were too wordy or too vague to help the audience follow the organization.	The presentation rambled with little evidence of an introduction, body, or conclusion. PowerPoints, overheads, or handouts were either not used or did not assist the audience in following the organization in any significant way.
Individual content 20%	Facts and examples were detailed, accurate, and appropriate. Theories referenced were accurately described and appropriately used. Analyses, discussions, and conclusions were explicitly linked to examples, facts, and theories.	Facts and examples were mostly detailed, accurate, and appropriate, but there were lapses. Theories were referenced, but they were either not accurately described or not appropriately used. The connection among analyses, discussions, and conclusions is evident or implied but not explicitly linked to examples, facts, and theories.	Facts and examples were seriously lacking in detail, inaccurate, or inappropriate. Theories referenced were inaccurately described and inappropriately used or not referenced or used at all. There was no clear connection among analyses, discussion, and examples, facts, and theories.

Figure 6.2 *Continued*

Presentation Rubric

Student: Stanley Livingston
Topic: Ad campaign

	Professional	Adequate	Needs work	You're fired	Grade
Content	Full grasp (more than needed) of material in initial presentations and in answering questions later.	Solid presentation of material and answers all questions adequately but without elaboration.	Less than a full grasp of the information revealed rudimentary presentation and answers to questions.	No grasp of information, some misinformation, and unable to answer questions accurately.	B+
Organization	Information is presented in a logical interesting sequence that is easy for the audience to follow.	Information is presented in a logical sequence that is easy for the audience to follow but a bit dull.	Presentation jumps around a lot and is not easy to follow, although it is possible.	Audience cannot follow presentations because they follow no logical sequence.	C
Graphics	Graphics explain and reinforce the rest of the presentation.	Graphics relate to the rest of the presentation.	Graphics are too few or not sufficiently related to the rest of the presentation.	Graphics are either not used or are superfluous.	B
English	No misspelled words or grammatical errors.	No more than two misspelled words or grammatical errors.	Three misspelled words or grammatical errors.	Four or more misspelled words or grammatical errors.	A
Elocution	Speaks clearly, correctly, and precisely, loud enough for audience to hear and slowly enough for easy understanding.	Speaks clearly, pronounces most words correctly, loud enough to be easily heard, and slow enough to be easily understood.	Speaks unclearly, mispronounces many major terms, and speaks too rapidly to be easily understood.	Mumbles, mispronounces most important terms, and speaks too softly or rapidly to be understood at all.	C
Eye Contact	Eye contact constant; minimal or no reading of notes.	Eye contact maintained except when consulting notes, which is too often.	Some eye contact, but mostly reading from notes.	No eye contact; reads from notes exclusively.	B–

Figure 6.3 Three-level rubric with circled feedback. Note how the less complex descriptions make this a viable way to grade using circles.

Scoring Guide Rubric for Film Presentations

Task Description: Prepare a one-hour presentation on an assigned film. You are expected to discuss how the film relates to the political, economic, or cultural aspects of the historical period it claims to depict and also the historiography of that era. You may also discuss it in terms of film theory if you wish.

FILM: *Black Rain*

Dimensions	Criteria	Comments
Introduction	The introduction tells the audience exactly what to expect in terms of how the speaker feels about the movie, what theories and theoretical framework(s) he or she will introduce, and what conclusions he or she will draw.	*All points covered succinctly. Used a PowerPoint to list the major points.*
Organization	The presentation is organized to create a logical argument and so that topics that need to be discussed together are presented together.	*Well ordered PowerPoints with clear captions show organization and connections.*
Context	The presenter discusses the main historical issues raised by the film and how other film scholars and historians have dealt with these issues both with regard to this film and in general. The presenter explains where he or she stands on these issues, which theories he or she finds most useful, and why.	*Discusses:* • *Shinto, Buddhism, death, and disease* • *Family and community patterns* • *Attitudes toward insanity (PTSD)* • *Novel and novelist* • *Reason for B/W choice*
Evidence	The presenter includes sufficient, detailed examples from the film and other sources to support her or his analyses.	*Approach was thematic with examples woven in.* *Video clips were short but effective.*
Analysis	The presenter uses her or his evidence to support a consistent, coherent analysis of how the film does or does not contribute to our understanding of World War II.	*Absolutely. A constant, elegantly complex analysis combining all elements listed previously in a scholarly way despite the speaker's evident emotional involvement.*
Presentation	The presenter spoke clearly, slowly, loudly enough to be heard, but not too loudly; used appropriate, effective gestures and body language; and maintained eye contact with the class. Audio-visual aids, if used, are technically sound (to prevent fumbling with equipment), appropriate, and referenced in the presentation.	*Excellent.*

1. Post-traumatic stress disorder
2. Black-and-white as opposed to color film

Figure 6.4 Scoring guide rubric with narrative feedback for a very good presentation.

specific ways in which the student had fulfilled these expectations, a more flexible option three- to five-level rubrics do not easily allow. The comments in the "Analysis" portion of the scoring guide rubric were pure applause, a way of expressing the professor's sheer delight in creativity and accomplishment that went beyond the highest expectations listed on the scoring guide rubric.

Scoring guide rubrics do not take much longer to use than three- to five-level rubrics when the work being graded is so strong. The greater time consumption occurs when the work does not come up to, or perhaps even close to, the highest levels of expectation listed on the scoring guide rubric. Then the lower levels of performance must be spelled out.

Figure 6.5 shows the same scoring guide rubric used in a different year for a weaker presentation on the same film in the same graduate seminar. As before, the professor's notes are in script.

In this case, the professor roughed out the notes as the student spoke, but she had to take them back to her office to elaborate (and to allow herself time to reflect on the work). The scoring guide rubric did not actually save much time. It made itemizing the nature of the student's weaknesses easier to organize, but the professor still had to write out in detail just precisely where, how, and to what extent the student had failed as well as succeeded in meeting expectations. It was also necessary to comment on the "creative and flexible" ways in which this student had "misunderstood" the assignment.

Fortunately, this sort of thing does not happen often in graduate classes where students are more motivated and can usually be expected to fulfill our expectations better than this, which is why scoring guide rubrics are usually preferred for upper-division and graduate classes. Even in cases where we are seriously disappointed in a student performance, however, the scoring guide rubric, like the three- to five-level rubrics, also saves us time simply by keeping us focused on what we are looking for as we grade and, of course, it also ensures greater consistency.

Summative Feedback: Assigning Grades

Then comes the moment of truth, the summing up, assigning grades or points. If we've quantified each dimension on the rubric, this can

Scoring Guide Rubric for Film Presentations

Task Description: Prepare a one-hour presentation on an assigned film. You are expected to discuss how the film relates to the political, economic, or cultural aspects of the historical period it claims to depict and also the historiography of that era. You may also discuss it in terms of film theory if you wish.

FILM: *Black Rain*

Dimensions	Criteria	Comments
Introduction	The introduction tells the audience exactly what to expect in terms of how the speaker feels about the movie, what theories and theoretical framework(s) she or he will introduce, and what conclusions she or he will draw.	*You did everything right except that you never mentioned the title of the movie. More seriously, although you included the fact that this movie is based on a novel, you never addressed this again.*
Organization	The presentation is organized to create a logical argument and so that topics that need to be discussed together are presented together.	*Dividing your historical research data from your analysis of the film itself weakened the impact of both and prevented you from noticing that your focus kept changing.*
Context	The presenter discusses the main historical issues raised by the film and how other film scholars and historians have dealt with these issues both with regard to this film and in general. The presenter explains where she or he stands on these issues, which theories she or he finds most useful, and why.	*Way too much focus on why America dropped the bomb. This is not actually a major issue in the movie or the novel. We needed to hear more about how accurately the movie shows the effects of the bombing, what it reveals about Japanese attitudes toward disease or marriage, and perhaps something about the stylistic elements that reveal Japanese artistic values. Some film theory might have helped with the latter. We also could have used more information on how this film is regarded both here and in Japan, such as reviews.*
Evidence	The presenter includes sufficient, detailed examples from the film and other sources to support her or his analyses.	*The research on effects of fallout was excellent, but you also needed to introduce specific examples from the film to support your contention that the film was accurate in depicting the progress of radiation illness. Some further introduction of scenes showing specific cultural elements (e.g., the twisted Jizo statues the shell-shocked soldier creates or the role of the mystic) would also have given you more to work with in your analysis.*
Analysis	The presenter uses her or his evidence to support a consistent, coherent analysis of how the film does or does not contribute to our understanding of World War II.	*Although your research focused mostly on the reasons America dropped the bomb and the effects of fallout, your analysis of the film focused on how the young soldier's story showed post-traumatic stress disorder. This is an interesting subplot, but it's still a subplot and you have not established any evidence or context to justify such a focus.*
Presentation	The presenter spoke clearly, slowly, and loudly enough to be heard, but not too loudly; used appropriate, effective gestures and body language; and maintained eye contact with the class. Audio-visual aids, if used, were technically sound (to prevent fumbling with equipment), appropriate, and referenced in the presentation.	*The clip from the army film showing the effects of the bomb was appropriate, but 20 minutes was too long for an hour-long presentation, especially since you only referenced it once or twice. Also, you were reading from your notes and looked up only rarely, and your voice was so soft it was difficult to hear you.*

Figure 6.5 Scoring guide rubric with narrative feedback for a weak presentation.

be a simple mathematical exercise. That was the case with the scoring guide rubric shown in Figure 6.6, which was used for a teacher education class in which students were to watch a non-Western film to deepen their understanding of diversity and present a creative response to the experience. Each item listed on the rubric was worth a set number of points; the professor provided a comment section to explain why a student might not be getting all points possible.

In addition, it should be noted that the rubric was created using the feedback model of collaborative rubric construction. The professor took the incomplete rubric into the classroom with the assignment on the top and the dimensions along the side but no descriptions for the dimensions. The students were divided into five groups. Each group wrote a series of descriptors for that dimension, and then the professor used those descriptions to create the final rubric. These descriptors were very meaningful to students. In fact, during the presentations, the professor noted that several students actually used the words "out of my comfort zone," a phrase also used on the rubric, to

<u>Creative Expressions—Adding Affirming Diversity 32 Points</u>
Scoring Rubric

Application of what we know and can learn from our increasingly diverse student population is imperative. Honestly facing our own biases and reactions and grappling with them is very important. The arts, in particular, provide an avenue of comprehension and expression that often reveal our deeper values. Thus, you are expected to do ONE of the following:

> Attend lecture by Sonja Nieto on January 16—take notes
> OR go to a non-English foreign film (subtitles), preferably not Western
> OR read a book furthering your understanding of diverse students or written
> by a person from another culture

Then create an expression of your response to this experience or otherness that relates somehow to the lecture or debate/discussion on themes in the class. This could be a POSTER, a POEM, a PIECE OF MUSIC, a PIECE OF ART, FOOD, or a STORY. To make the connection to the class clear to other audiences, either add a written narrative piece to the work or tell us how this directly relates to the class.

Dimension	Description	Comment	Points
Topic and outline 3 pts.	☑ Paragraph description of project turned in on time ☐ Details of project, type of project ☐ Link to class topic clear	*Unclear if it's a movie or a book at heart of project.* *No mention of diversity*	1

Figure 6.6   Collaboratively constructed scoring guide rubric with check boxes and narrative feedback.

Dimension	Description	Comment	Points
Content: 8 pts. Karen Dianas Jana Gwenda Tanya Denise Chisa Karen Jennifer	☑ Clear focus of project—what lecture, reading, movie inspired the idea ☑ Grabs attention right from the beginning ❑ Identifies a significant cultural difference ❑ Describes values of that difference to the culture ❑ Describes how you viewed previous assumptions of the culture ☑ Includes brief summary of the movie, book ☑ Describes clear purpose behind this choice ❑ Clear connection to adding/affirming diversity	*No discussion of previous assumptions Cultural differences described but not recognized as such Diversity never mentioned; focus on artistic expression.*	4
Organization: 5 pts. Lori Sheila Debbie Tanya Julie	☑ Clear beginning, middle, end ☑ Understandable to others, not confusing ☑ Clear directions and wrap up ❑ Easy to see connections to adding/affirming diversity ❑ Clear link to class topics	*Well-written short story, but still no mention of topic diversity.*	3
Creativity: 11 pts. Lori Gwenda Sherrie Tanya Chisa Bobbi Jennifer Brad	❑ Puts together a presentation that is "out of your comfort zone" ☑ Expresses emotional response ☑ Open/honest ☑ Attractive ☑ Visually pleasing ☑ Creates at least half of the images ☑ Obvious extra effort (not copied pages) ☑ Authenticity and uniqueness of effort ☑ Thought provoking ☑ Original ❑ Strong expression of "otherness"	*Stuck to recognizable relationships and situations, ignoring those not understood or related to. Strong expression of universality, also a valid perception, but not the point of the assignment.*	9
Reflection: 2 pts. Bobbi Brad	❑ Indicates how your perceptions and assumptions have changed ❑ Indicates how this might affect your future teaching and adding/affirming diversity in your life	*Lack of previous assumption discussion prevents comparison. No direct reference to educational implications.*	0
Conventions: 3 pts. Sheila Chisa Gwenda	☑ All grammar, spelling, punctuation correct ☑ Neatly presented ☑ If typed, double-spaced and pages numbered		3

Figure 6.6 *Continued*

describe what they did on the assignment. The student names were put on the rubric to honor their individual contributions in creating the rubric. Quantifying in this way is often reassuring to students because it reveals priorities so well. By weighing the dimensions differently, it shows that the dimensions are not all equal in importance. And using numbers, of course, makes it is easier to come up with a final grade.

The professor also found that this scoring guide rubric, with its assigned point system, made it easier to keep the differential weights of the dimensions in proper perspective when grading. The professor realized that she was often disproportionately affected by mistakes in spelling, sometimes allowing them to overshadow creative content in some students' work. Using the scoring guide rubric, however, she was reminded each time that such conventions were worth only 3 points, while content was worth 10 points, almost a third of the total points possible.

She also found that even giving conventions 3 points seemed to capture student attention to those details in a way that a mere description in the syllabus did not. Thus, the scoring guide rubric not only made her grading faster, fairer, and more focused, but it produced student work less likely to offend her eyes.

Quantification like this increases students' perception (and our intention) that we are being impartial, but it also makes it less likely that the students will be in during office hours to argue over 1 or 2 points. In this case, however, the professor could simply point to the names of the students who created the criteria, a tactic that most students accepted as validation of the rubric.

In other cases, however, concerns about those whining arguments over points is why some of us may not quantify the various dimensions of the rubric. Remember that before we used rubrics, the only feedback we gave were narrative comments and a letter grade. Now we have detailed descriptions of an exemplary performance with scoring guide rubrics and even more details when we use the three- to five-level rubric. Those descriptions are rich feedback to students even without quantitative grades.

The grid format also allows those of us who prefer to base our final grade on holistic judgments on the work as a whole to do so more quickly and more consistently. The three-level rubric for the group film report in Freshman Inquiry shown in Figure 6.7 contained no quantitative information. In this case, the professor simply checked off all the relevant categories, added a few circles for clarification, then added up how many checks were in each column. With nine checks in the Exemplary column and five in the Competent column, it was immediately clear that this would be an A− or B+ paper. Another quick glance at the circles revealed that the objections mostly related to only one aspect of at least three dimension descriptions. The professor paused for a moment, considered the impact of the overall paper, and made it an A−.

Grading Our Own Teaching Methods

We professors reflect on or "grade" our own teaching as we grade the students' papers. For many of us, this is just a matter of making mental notes on what worked and what didn't, or perhaps a muttered "I'm never doing this again." Some of us go further and write notes to ourselves. But those of us who routinely use rubrics to grade student work sometimes find ourselves using rubrics to grade our own teaching.

These rubrics are generally laconic because we know what we mean and these, after all, are for our own feedback. Figure 6.8, for example, shows a simple rubric used to summarize how students completed a major assignment, a research paper, in a class in early Japanese history. As the professor read through the papers and calculated the students' grades, she simply checked off where she felt her students ranked in their accomplishment of specific learning goals and understanding of the discipline; the professor's notes are in script.

By identifying her own hopes for her students learning in advance and checking off what she did and did not find in the papers she was grading, the professor easily and quickly created a permanent record she will use the next time she teaches this class. This is a quick and easy way to check the link between course objectives and student learning and ultimately to improve classroom instruction. It also provided meaningful feedback on the overall class performance that was shared with the students as the papers were handed back.

Rubric for Film Presentation

Task Description: Working in groups of four or five, students will develop and present to the class an analysis of a Japanese movie about World War II. This analysis should go beyond a simple synopsis of the movie to discuss how well or poorly the film reflects a particular point of view about the war. You are expected to do additional research to develop this presentation and to use visual aids of some sort. All group members are expected to participate in the presentation.

Dimension	Exemplary	Competent	Developing
Individual presentation skills	☐ The presenter spoke clearly, slowly, and loudly enough to be heard without shouting, and modulated voice tone and quality.	☑ The presenter was understood but mumbled, spoke fast or too slow, whispered shouted, or droned; intelligibility, however, was not compromised.	☐ The presenter mumbled, spoke too fast or too slow, whispered or shouted, or droned to the point where intelligibility was compromised.
	☑ The presenter used expressive, appropriate body language and maintained eye contact with the audience.	☑ The presenter's body language did not distract significantly, but the presenter fidgeted, remained rigid, never looked at the audience, or engaged in other inappropriate body language.	☐ The presenter fidgeted, remained rigid, never looked at the audience, or engaged in other body language that distracted seriously from the content.
	☐ The presenter used all the time allotted but did not speak too long.	☑ The presenter's timing was (too long) or too brief.	☐ The presenter barely used the time allotted of used much too much time.
	☑ The presenter used humor and anecdotes appropriately to liven up and illustrate the presentation.	☐ Humor and anecdotes were used, but they were over- or underused to liven up and or illustrate the presentation.	☐ The lack of humor and anecdotes made the presentation dull.
	☑ The presenter or an assistant competently handled the equipment.	☐ Equipment was used, but there was some fumbling although not to the point where it seriously distracted from the presentation.	☐ There was a lot of fumbling with the equipment that could have been prevented with a little practice.
Group presentation skills	☑ The presentation allowed each member an equal opportunity to shine.	☐ The presentation was unbalanced in the way time or content was assigned to members.	☐ The presentation was seriously unbalanced so that one or a few people dominated and or carried the ball.
	☐ The individual presentations followed one another in a way that promoted a logical discussion of the topic, and connections between individual presentations were clearly shown.	☑ The individual presentations followed one another in a way that mostly promoted a logical discussion of the topic, but connections between individual presentations were not clearly shown, or the presentation lost direction from time to time for other reasons.	☐ There was little if any evident logic in bow the individual presentations followed one another, and the connections between individual presentations were unclear.
	☑ Group members treated each other with courtesy and respect.	☐ Group members mostly treated each other with courtesy and respect, but there were lapses where members were not listening to each other.	☐ Group members showed little respect or courtesy toward one another.

Figure 6.7 Three-level rubric with checked boxes for summative feedback and grading.

Dimension	Exemplary	Competent	Developing
Group organization	☑ The group thesis is clearly stated at the beginning and carried through in the rest of the presentation. ☐ The topics to be covered are introduced and the direction the overall presentation will take is made clear.	☐ The group thesis emerges from the presentation but is either unclear, unstated, or not stated directly. ☐ A clear thesis is stated, but it is not carried through in the presentation. ☑ Topics to be covered and the direction the presentation will take are stated but they are not the topics covered or the direction actually taken.	☐ There is no stated group thesis. ☐ There is no indication of what topics will be covered or what direction that coverage will take. ☐ No order or focus emerges in the course of the presentation.
Individual organization	☑ The individual presentation was well organized in itself with an introduction, body, and conclusion. ☐ That organization was emphasized and made clear to the audience through the use of appropriately captioned PowerPoints, overheads, and/or handouts.	☑ The individual presentation was mostly well organized, but there were problems with the introduction, body, or conclusion. ☑ The presenter used (PowerPoints,) overheads, handouts, but those were (too wordy) or too vague to help the audience follow the organization.	☐ The presentation rambled with little evidence of an introduction, body, or conclusion. ☐ PowerPoints, overheads, or handouts either were not used or did not assist the audience in following the organization in any significant way.
Individual content	☑ Facts and examples were detailed, accurate, and appropriate. ☑ Theories referenced were accurately described and appropriately used. ☐ Analyses, discussions, and conclusions were explicitly linked to examples, facts, and theories.	☐ Facts and examples were mostly detailed, accurate, and appropriate, but there were lapses. ☐ Theories were referenced but they were either not accurately described or not appropriately used. ☑ The connection among analyses, discussions, and conclusions is evident or (implied, but it is (not explicitly linked to) examples, facts, and theories.	☐ Facts and examples were seriously lacking in detail, inaccurate, or inappropriate. ☐ Theories referenced were inaccurately described and inappropriately used or not referenced or used at all. ☐ There is no clear connection among analyses, discussions, and examples, facts, and theories.

Figure 6.7   *Continued*

Class: Hist. Early Japan

Assignment objectives	What students did on various aspects of the assignment	What I can do next time—changes in instruction and this assignment
Content	Names, dates, and events are ❑ Accurate ✓✓✓ ❑ Mostly accurate ✓✓✓✓ ❑ Inaccurate ✓✓✓✓✓✓✓ They are used: ❑ Appropriately ✓✓✓✓✓✓ ❑ Mostly appropriately ✓✓✓ ✓✓✓✓ ❑ Inappropriately ✓✓✓	*Give more quizzes. Looks like they're doing the research for the assigned work but not the general class reading.*
Research	Used: Internet✓✓✓✓✓✓✓✓✓ ✓✓✓✓ Books✓✓✓✓✓✓✓✓✓✓✓ Journals✓✓✓✓✓✓ Databases✓ Primary documents✓✓	*Watch their references. May need to allow no more than three Internet sources.* *Add class period in library to learn databases.* *Do class exercise using primary sources.*
Historiography	Recognize authorial biases ✓✓ ✓✓✓✓✓✓✓✓✓✓ Recognize different schools ✓✓ ✓✓✓✓✓✓✓✓✓✓✓	*I think they've got it!*
Writing skills	Understand what a book critique is and can write one ✓ ✓✓✓✓✓✓✓✓✓✓✓✓✓ Understand what a research paper is and can write one ✓✓ ✓✓✓✓✓✓✓✓✓✓ Know when and how to cite sources ✓✓✓✓✓✓✓✓✓✓ ✓✓✓✓✓	*My tirade on citations seems to be working, and so are the grading rubrics for the papers.*

Figure 6.8   Rubric used by instructor to summarize how students completed the assignment.

Evaluating Our Own Rubrics: Metarubrics

Rubrics are not cast in cement. They are flexible, adaptable grading tools that become better and better the more times we use them. Their strength, reliability, and validity increase as we use rubrics, discover limitations, and make revisions. But to make effective revisions, we first need to evaluate our existing rubrics.

A "metarubric" is a rubric used to evaluate rubrics. Some of us use a metarubric to evaluate a new rubric before showing it to our students. Some of us use metarubrics to reevaluate old rubrics after using them to grade a set of assignments, especially if that grading proved unsatisfactory in some way.

Like our evaluations of our assignments, metarubrics are for our own use and tend to be individual. Checklists are easier and quicker to use. When we use the metarubric, we glance back and forth from the rubric to the metarubric criteria. It helps refine and polish some of the details in the rubric. Figure 6.9 is a metarubric developed by some faculty in the Graduate School of Education at Portland State University. The "yes/no" element allows for a quick check on key aspects of rubric construction without belaboring the details.

Conclusion

In this chapter we discussed and demonstrated the use of rubrics as a grading tool and as a form of self-assessment. Methods of using rubrics can and do vary, but on the whole, the checking, circling, and commenting methods described are the most commonly used.

Metarubric

Rubric Part	Evaluation Criteria	Yes	No
The dimensions	Does each dimension cover important parts of the final student performance?		
	Does the dimension capture some key themes in your teaching?		
	Are the dimensions clear?		
	Are the dimensions distinctly different from each other?		
	Do the dimensions represent skills that the student knows something about already (e.g., organization, analysis, using conventions)?		
The descriptions	Do the descriptions match the dimensions?		
	Are the descriptions clear and different from each other?		
	If you used points, is there a clear basis for assigning points for each dimension?		
	If using a three- to five-level rubric, are the descriptions appropriately and equally weighted across the three- to five-level levels?		
The scale	Do the descriptors under each level truly represent that level of performance?		
	Are the scale labels (e.g., exemplary, competent, beginning) encouraging and still quite informative without being negative and discouraging?		
	Does the rubric have a reasonable number of levels for the age of the student and the complexity of the assignment?		
The overall rubric	Does the rubric clearly connect to the outcomes that it is designed to measure?		
	Can the rubric be understood by external audiences (avoids jargon and technical language)?		
	Does it reflect teachable skills?		
	Does the rubric reward or penalize students based on skills unrelated to the outcome being measured that you have not taught?		
	Have all students had an equal opportunity to learn the content and skills necessary to be successful on the assignment?		
	Is the rubric appropriate for the conditions under which the assignment was completed?		
	Does the rubric include the assignment description or title?		
	Does the rubric address the student's performance as a developmental task?		
	Does the rubric inform the student about the evaluation procedures when his or her work is scored?		
	Does the rubric emphasize the appraisal of individual or group performance and indicate ways to improve?		
Fairness and sensibility	Does it look like the rubric will be fair to all students and free of bias?		
	Does it look like it will be useful to students as performance feedback?		
	Is the rubric practical given the kind of assignment?		
	Does the rubric make sense to the reader?		

Figure 6.9   Metarubric. How to evaluate the overall quality of your rubric.

7

MAKING IT YOURS

Finding ready-made rubrics isn't difficult; this book is filled with them. Colleagues are often happy to share their rubrics. There are departmental rubrics on file, program-specific rubrics, and often even campus-wide rubrics; some of these are for grading, but more are designed for program assessment. And then there's the Internet: Rubi-Star, iRubric, Kathy Schrock's Guide for Educators, and so on. What's wrong with all these rubrics? Absolutely nothing. Except that they're not yours.

If rubrics are to grade accurately and fairly, if they are to convey your scholarly expectations of your students, they need to be yours. They need to reflect what you already know about this task, what you deem to be important, and what you will consider as you judge each student's work. In this chapter, we look at how what we will call "ready-made rubrics" can be modified so they are truly yours.

Should You Use Ready-Made Rubrics at All?

There are certainly good reasons to look at other people's rubrics. If they were useless, we would not have included so many in this book. Aside from including them to illustrate our approach to rubrics and showing the possible variations in how rubrics are made, the examples we have included also offer suggestions regarding language that works well in descriptions of dimensions and in describing levels of performance. You cannot, however, use them as is, not even if you are using them on very similar assignments. Only you know what you truly want from your students and what kind of feedback you think they need to receive on their work. You already knew that. In fact, you probably made changes in your head as you read through the ready-made rubrics we provided.

Whether it makes sense to use a ready-made rubric depends on two related issues: time and suitability.

Time

Does using a ready-made rubric save you time? First, there is the matter of finding the rubric. Sometimes it's a colleague's rubric that appears in your e-mail. That takes no time at all, and if it's at all suitable, is well worth looking at. If, however, no one is handing you a rubric, you might want to consider whether it might not be easier to make your own rubric from scratch rather than spend time searching for one and then revising it. Here, too, the closer to home you can go, the less time you're likely to spend. If your department maintains a rubric archive on its website, or even an old-fashioned filing cabinet stuffed with old rubrics, that's a quick and easy stop and likely to yield rubrics suitable enough to meet your needs.

If, however, you go to a more general website like RubiStar or iRubric, you may spend hours searching through the offerings before you find one that can even provide a basis for the kind of rubric you need. Most of the rubrics on these sites come from K–12 teachers and are not designed for higher education at all, so be prepared to check out numerous titles that turn out to be intended for eight-year-olds.

Departmental, program, or university rubrics designed for assessment may not be appropriate for your own classroom objectives, albeit in different ways. They are often readily available and can provide food for thought, but typically they are not designed for grading course assignments, so the amount of time required for adaptation is likely to be considerable.

Suitability

The same questions of closeness of fit that apply to time spent also apply to suitability. The closer to home you can go to find rubrics, the better. This relates both to the question of immediate suitability to the specific assignment, and to a more general suitability for departmental and sometimes even campus-wide approaches to learning goals.

As with the question of time, a colleague's rubric developed for a similar or identical assignment for a similar or identical class is the most suitable to your needs. The same is true for archived rubrics, provided they are fairly recent. Such rubrics have the added benefit that their original creators are likely to be available to answer questions and offer information on how well they worked.

Professors who share rubrics, either by borrowing them from or lending them to colleagues, often find that this offers a side benefit in that it necessarily entails sharing educational goals and approaches. Departments and programs that aspire to some sort of shared mission or team teaching often use rubrics and rubric creation as a means to that end. Even in departments that have no such explicit goals, professors who share rubrics often find they are discussing their teaching styles and objectives in the process.

To some degree, this is also true of using program assessment rubrics. Program assessment rubrics are usually quite unsuitable to grading needs. This is not what they are designed for; it's as simple as that. What they can do, however, is provide you with long-term goals, the overall student learning outcomes (SLOs) your department or program or even a campus-wide assessment committee is hoping for. That purpose can guide how you develop and grade your assignments, but you still have to provide the specifics of what parts of that overall goal you want any particular assignment to address. (Chapter 12 details the hows and whys of using rubrics in program assessment.)

Using Online Rubrics

Rubrics found online are far more problematic. Their biggest problem, from your point of view, is that most of them are designed for K–12 classes. They can sometimes supply more playful ideas that college students appreciate as much as do the younger students for whom they were created. This is especially true in the words used for levels. One grade school teacher, for example, uses "Unbelievable!" for her highest level of achievement, while another features emoticons rather than words. You may want to consider including some of that playfulness and humor in your rubrics if it suits your style.

However, K–12 rubrics, and even the few higher education rubrics found on websites like RubiStar and iRubric, are unlikely to be ready-made for your highest levels of performance. You may eventually find high school rubrics or even some higher education offerings that suit your needs to some degree, but these will require far more modifications than ones you borrow from colleagues.

Another issue is that few of these websites include task descriptions, which are an essential part of understanding the context in which the rubric was designed. A rubric designed for an unknown task is of limited value. Of course, you can e-mail the creators of these rubrics to ask, but here, too, you are looking at a more time-consuming process.

The Four Stages of Rubric Modification

However you find or decide to use a ready-made rubric, you will almost certainly be modifying it to some degree, using much the same four stages you would have used had you created your own rubric from scratch. The ready-made rubric does not replace this process. It can provide a focus and ideas, but ultimately the assignment is yours, so the rubric should be yours, too. It should reflect what you want and how you grade, and it should convey that information to your students.

With that in mind and a ready-made rubric in hand, here are a few ways you can make the necessary modifications using the same four stages you would have used in devising a rubric from scratch.

Stage 1: Reflecting

Whether you begin with the ready-made rubric or without it depends on how suitable you judge it to be as is. If you are using a colleague's rubric created for a similar or identical task and context, you may want to keep the rubric in mind as you consider the questions listed on pages 30–32.

1. *Why did you create this assignment?* You might add to this question, Why is your assignment so similar to that created by the colleague from whom you borrowed the rubric? Is this a case of great minds thinking alike? Did you also borrow the assignment and probably the syllabus from this colleague? If so, why did this colleague create this assignment? If that's not obvious to you, ask. If you can't ask and it's still not obvious, perhaps you should recon-sider the whole thing.

2. *Have you given this assignment or a similar assignment before?* Unless this is your very first teaching experience, you probably have, so review what happened the last time. If you have never

given this assignment before, and/or if you borrowed it along with the rubric, you might ask the colleague you borrowed it from. Either way, consider what you hoped it would teach your students and how well or poorly it accomplished that. Now look at the rubric. Does it reflect those hopes and warn against those common mistakes? If it doesn't, perhaps it's not suitable for you.

3. *How does this assignment relate to the rest of what you are teaching?* Here, too, it's a good idea to think about it first, and then consult the rubric you have borrowed. Even if it's an excellent rubric from a similar assignment, its focus and expectations may be different from the overall goals you have for your class.

4. *What skills will students need to have or develop to complete this assignment successfully?* This, too, is about context in overall course objectives. Here, too, you might want to consider the matter first, and then apply your musings to the rubric in hand to see how well it actually corresponds.

5. *What exactly is the task assigned? And how does it break down into smaller, individual tasks?* Unless the ready-made rubric you are considering is for an identical assignment, you need to check carefully how the rubric divides the tasks into dimensions that fit what you are assigning. Even if the assignment is identical, it's a good idea to check this.

6. *What evidence can students provide in this assignment that will show they have accomplished what you hoped they would accomplish when you created the assignment?* Here, too, your idea of evidence may be different from the original creator of the rubric, so consider it carefully. Are there demands in the descriptions of the dimensions that you consider questionable? Are there omissions of things that you would consider important?

7. *What are the highest expectations you have for student performance on this assignment overall?* Did the original author of your ready-made rubric have the same expectations you do? If not, you'll need to change the rubric.

8. *What is the worst quality of performance of the assignment you can imagine, short of simply not turning it in at all?* It's easy to overlook the last column of the rubric, the one you have labeled

"Needs Work," "Novice," or something like that, but it's just as important as your highest expectations. In this column, you not only warn your students away from common mistakes students make, but you also alert them to your own pet peeves, like your preference for correct grammar and spelling, or even the fact that you get annoyed if pages are out of order and not numbered. And if those details listed in the original rubric are different from yours, they will need to be changed, too.

If the rubric is seriously unsuitable in some ways, you may prefer to put it out of your mind until you reach Stage 2, Listing or Stage 3, Grouping and Labeling.

Stage 2: Listing

Once you have considered these questions, it's time to start listing, putting things down on paper. When creating a rubric from scratch, this takes the form of lists of learning objectives and highest expectations based on your reflections. When you are working with an existing rubric, it may take a messier form with crossed-out and/or highlighted sections and, if you are using the original rubric at this stage, balloons featuring suggested insertions into the original rubric as well as lists.

At this point you may begin to wonder if using a ready-made rubric is saving you as much time and work as you hoped. And it's at this point that you need to be especially careful that the existing rubric does not overly influence you. After all, it looks so tidy and well-organized, so official, while your scrawls, lists, and inserts are so obviously a work in progress. But that work in progress reflects your actual expectations, while the tidy boxes of the original rubric do not. The learning objectives and highest expectations it will ultimately reflect must be yours. And it will all look tidier, more organized, and more official once you reach the end of the process.

That doesn't mean you should never be influenced by the existing rubric. Using a ready-made rubric can also be a way to jog your mind into recognizing things you may never have put into words. Provided you can justify including new ideas and material, this can be useful.

In the same way, you might also consider using departmental or even campus-wide assessment rubrics if those exist. Although using such rubrics is unlikely to save much time because they will require extensive adaptation, this is a good way to ensure that your individual rubric, created for a particular assignment, also reflects the learning objectives of your overall institution. It is important, though, that your own views, especially those reflecting the individual assignment, are truly your own.

Stage 3: Grouping and Labeling

This is where using a ready-made rubric really will save you time. You already have your grid in the form of the ready-made rubric, and if you have used a ready-made rubric in Stage 2, as many as two rubrics suitably highlighted and annotated. And now you have your own notes, lists, and margin scribbles.

It is tempting at this point to simply start editing the existing ready-made rubric, especially if you have it in Word, but this is not advisable. This is not something that is best done in the abstract. Whether you use Post-its, index cards, or some other sort of written or typed lists, it is better to transfer all of those jottings into a new form. Then continue to group and label them as you would when making a rubric from scratch. This may take a little extra time, but it's worth it. Typing bits into an existing format sometimes means you will overlook alternate possibilities and connections. Start with a new grid as you move on to Stage 4, Application.

Stage 4: Application

Rewriting is also a good idea when creating your final rubric. Here, too, it is tempting to simply use the existing grid winking at you so seductively from your screen, but things go more smoothly if you start with a new grid. You can cut and paste the bits that still work from the original, but we suggest doing this sparingly. Rewriting and retyping quite often leads to productive reconfigurations that would not otherwise occur.

Case Study

Eduardo, a professor teaching in the freshman core program at Portland State University borrowed an assignment description and the rubric for grading it from Mia, a colleague. Figure 1.6 on page 12 is the rubric for the "Changing Communities in Our City" oral presentation task. He initially chose it because he felt his assignments so far had focused on document-based research. He liked the idea of students doing something more hands-on, creating their own data.

Reflection

The first thing Eduardo noticed about the borrowed rubric in the course of his reflections was that it had been designed for work done during the first term of Mia's class. Therefore, she had focused heavily on presentation skills and basic scholarly research techniques. His class was now in the final term of its yearlong class, and students had already done two oral presentations and written three scholarly papers. They didn't really need that much emphasis on developing such skills.

The second thing Eduardo noticed was that the task description didn't really include doing original research. It read:

> Each student will make a 5-minute presentation on the changes in one Portland community over the past 30 years. The student may focus the presentation in any way he or she wishes. Students need to develop a thesis of some sort, not just a chronological exposition. The presentation should include appropriate photographs, maps, graphs, and other visual aids for the audience.

At the end of his reflections, before even beginning the listing process, Eduardo rewrote the task description:

> Each student will make a 5-minute presentation on independent research focusing on one Portland community. Such independent research can take the form of a survey, interviews, or attending community events. The presentation should include appropriate data drawn from other sources, but the focus should be the student's own observations, data collection, and interpretation.

Also in the course of his reflections, he thought about how this assignment would relate not only to the overall goals for the class, but also to the stated Four Goals of University Studies, the agreed-upon goals of the entire freshman core faculty. As he considered that, he looked back over his previous syllabi and concluded that, although this year he had done a fairly good job covering three of those goals (Communication, Critical Thinking, and the Diversity of Human Experience), he felt he had not adequately addressed the fourth: Ethical Issues and Social Responsibility.

It occurred to him that this assignment might be a good place to include that, so he pulled out the assessment rubric that had been created for the program's annual review of randomly selected student portfolios. See the assignment rubric in Figure 7.1.

This rubric was never designed for grading individual students; instead, it was meant to reflect how the program expects students to develop over time, meaning over the four years of college. It is used in an annual assessment in which randomly selected portfolios from the freshman core are rated to determine how well the program as a whole is meeting its goals. (The University Studies assessment rubrics are discussed more fully in Chapter 12; the full set of assessment rubrics is in Appendices E–I.) In this case, however, it provided Eduardo with a clear definition of "ethical values and social responsibility" and some suggestions for how students might demonstrate that they had a good grasp of that subject.

Because the Ethical Issues and Social Responsibility rubric had also been developed to cover the totality of a 4-year program, Eduardo, like the assessors, focused his listing on the criteria found in level 4 in the rubric. For freshmen at the end of their first year, a "4" would be an exemplary score. It reminded him that his rubric was to be an honest expression of what he could realistically expect from his students. He came to realize that all too often he made rubrics that reflected some sort of Platonic ideal or, worse yet, some expectations that were attempts to reassure himself of his own high standards rather than to guide his students to successful task completion. Once he realized that, he altered his listings accordingly. Later on, he also changed some of his other grading rubrics!

Listing

Armed with the original rubric borrowed from his colleague, the program assessment rubric from the program, and his own draft rewrite

Ethical Issues and Social Responsibility

Note: In this scoring guide, the phrase "ethical issues and social responsibility" refers to the impact and value of individuals and their choices on society—intellectually, socially, and personally.

6 (highest)	Portfolio creatively and comprehensively articulates approaches to ethical issues and social responsibility, in a scholarly manner, citing specific evidence. Demonstrates an ability to view multiple sides of these issues, to question what is being taught, and to construct independent meaning and interpretations.
	Portfolio presents well-developed ideas on the role of ethical issues and social responsibility in both private and public life. Demonstrates a deep awareness of how a conceptual understanding of ethical issues and social responsibility manifests concretely in one's own personal choices, including decisions on when and how to act.
5	Portfolio analyzes ethical issues and social responsibility in a scholarly manner and makes thoughtful connections between this area of study and its effects on lives, ideas, and events.
	Portfolio discusses explicitly how a deepening understanding of ethical issues and social responsibility has influenced personal opinions, decisions, and views on the role of self in society.
4	Portfolio thoughtfully analyzes, in a scholarly manner, a situation or situations in which ethical issues and social responsibility have played an important role. Begins to investigate connections between areas of controversy and to extrapolate meaning from specific examples.
	Portfolio applies learning in ethical issues and social responsibility to issues that arise in everyday life, and contemplates the impact of personal ethical choices and social action in the context of interpersonal and broader societal spheres.
3	Portfolio exhibits a working knowledge of major themes and scholarly debates surrounding ethical issues and social responsibility, and applies this understanding to some topic(s), but offers no independent analysis.
	References ethical issues and social responsibility as a subject of personal inquiry, begins to question established views, and contemplates in some way the value and impact of individual choices and personal action on one's broader community.
2	Portfolio mentions some issue(s) involving ethics and/or talks about social responsibility in a general fashion, but does not discuss these areas in a meaningful way.
	Portfolio contains some evidence of self-reflection in the area of ethical issues and/or social responsibility, but this reflection is superficial and reveals little or no questioning of established views.
1 (lowest)	Portfolio displays little or no engagement with the subjects of ethical issues and social responsibility.
	Demonstrates little or no recognition of ethical issues and social responsibility as subjects worthy of personal inquiry.

X = No Basis for Scoring (use only for missing or malfunctioning portfolios)

Figure 7.1   Program assessment rubric for Ethical and Social Responsibility, University Studies, Portland State University.

of the assignment, Eduardo then began listing his learning goals on separate sheets of paper. In doing so, he noticed that he often borrowed language from both rubrics.

Eduardo then progressed to listing more specific expectations for performance on Post-its. He was surprised to discover that they were markedly different from those on the borrowed rubric and did not offer his students any hint of his hope that they would demonstrate ethical standards and social responsibility in this assignment. Accordingly, he added two new lines to the task description:

> Students will address ethical issues and social responsibility in how they conduct their research and explicitly include appropriate ethical and social issues in their interpretation of their research.

Grouping and Labeling

Once Eduardo began grouping his Post-its, the difference between the rubric he wanted and the borrowed rubric grew even greater. He had assumed that he would use most of the original dimensions. He expected to add one dimension covering the ethics component, and thought he might compress the oral presentation criteria into one single dimension with a lesser weight.

Once Eduardo had grouped his Post-its, however, he realized that all but one, Communication, had changed. Knowledge/Understanding had become Scholarly Support, and he added a whole new Independent Research dimension as well as one for Ethical Issues (Figure 7.2).

He also changed the title, removing the word "changing" since that was no longer the focus of the assignment, and allowed each student 10 minutes instead of the original 5.

One other change related to his syllabus, although it came about as a result of the changes to the rubric. As he spelled out his expectations in the rubric, he realized how much he was asking of his students and that it was much more than Mia, the colleague from whom he had borrowed the rubric, had expected. He realized that he should drop a shorter paper in the class so that students could put more effort into this important assignment.

Application

In the end, Eduardo's new rubric looked like Figure 7.2. The changes were so great that he initially wondered why he'd even bothered to borrow a rubric. In fact, it might have been quicker to make his own. On the other hand, he acknowledged that using two other rubrics had triggered ideas and concepts he might not have had on his own. Even more important, he realized that by incorporating ideas drawn from Mia's rubric and the program assessment rubric, he had produced a composite that not only reflected his own aspirations for his students, but also was something that connected his teaching and his assignment to the overall educational aspirations of the University Studies program. The result, he concluded, was richer than anything he could have produced by himself.

Conclusion

Using "ready-made rubrics" gathered from the Internet or colleagues or an old, dusty file cabinet does have its advantages. You can borrow phrases and ideas from the descriptions of the dimensions. You can see how others have labeled the levels of performance. It can be a launching pad for your own rubric. And as enticing as these other rubrics are, do not forget that there are two major considerations when seeking to "borrow" another rubric: time and suitability. Will you have the time to adapt and modify the rubric for your own uses? In addition, how suitable is the rubric for the task you are having students complete?

Communities in Our City

Task Description: Each student will make a 10-minute presentation on independent research focusing on one Portland community. Such independent research can take the form of a survey, interviews, or attending community events. The presentation should be the student's own observations, data collection, and interpretation. Students will demonstrate awareness of ethical standards and social responsibility in how they conduct their research and explicitly include appropriate ethical and social issues in their interpretation of their research.

	Excellent	Competent	Needs Work
Ethical issues: 30%	Presenter clearly identifies major areas of ethical concern and controversy related to the community, and identifies the impact these have on his or her personal ethical choices and social action decisions.	Presenter identifies some areas of ethical concern and controversy related to the community, and touches on the impact these have on his or her personal ethical choices and social action decisions.	Presenter inadequately identifies areas of ethical concern and controversy related to the community, and offers little if any insight into the impact of these on his or her personal ethical choices and social action decisions.
Independent research: 30%	Research project is original and based on historiographic or social issues specific to the community. Analysis of the data collected is objective and conclusions are clearly stated.	Research project is based on historiographic or social issues specific to the community, but offers few new insights or angles into topics of concern. Analysis of the data collected is mostly objective, but conclusions could go further or be stated more clearly.	Connection of the research project to historiographic or social issues specific to the community is unclear and/or not cited. Analysis of the data collected is seriously undermined by biases or unrelated to the data. Conclusions are absent or confusing.
Scholarly support: 15%	The project undertaken is clearly shown to be based on ongoing and previously conducted research and analyses, and these are explicitly cited. Ethical issues are also explicitly related to existing philosophical, religious, or other contexts.	The project undertaken is based on ongoing and previously conducted research and analyses, but the connection is not explicitly cited. Ethical issues are somewhat related to existing philosophical, religious, or other contexts but how and why is not always clear.	The project undertaken does not seem to be based on ongoing and previously conducted research and analyses, and none is explicitly cited. Ethical issues are ignored or expressed as personal opinions that are not explicitly related to existing philosophical, religious, or other contexts.
Communication: 15%	The presentation is centered around an explicitly stated thesis. Creative and effective visual aids are used to show results and patterns, and are referenced at appropriate moments. Questions are solicited and answered in ways that show thought and knowledge beyond what was originally presented.	The presentation is centered around a thesis, although this is not always clearly stated or adhered to. Clear and accurate visual aids are used to show results and patterns, and are referenced at least some of the time. Questions are solicited and answered adequately, although in ways that do not add anything new.	The presentation does not seem to have a thesis. Visual aids are absent, unclear, or otherwise fail to show results and patterns: whatever is used is not referenced much or at all in the course of the presentation. Questions are either not solicited or are answered in ways that are inaccurate, irrelevant, or show that the presenter did not listen to the question.
Presentation skills: 10%	The presenter speaks clearly, loudly enough to be heard but not too loud, and not too fast or too slowly. Eye contact, a lively tone, gestures, and body language are all used to engage the audience.	The presenter does all of the following except one: speaks clearly, loudly enough to be heard but not too loud, and not too fast or too slowly. The presenter uses all but one of the following: eye contact, a lively tone, gestures, and body language.	The presenter fails to do two or more of the following: speaks clearly, loudly enough to be heard but not too loud, and not too fast or too slowly. The presenter fails to use two or more of the following: eye contact, a lively tone, gestures, and body language.

Figure 7.2 Eduardo's rubric for oral presentation that includes ethical and social responsibility components.

8

RUBRICS FOR LEARNING FROM EXPERIENCE

What I hear, I forget.
What I see, I remember.
What I do, I understand.
CHINESE PROVERB

Doing something teaches more than simply talking about it or even showing it. That is perhaps best demonstrated in the sciences where lab sessions are routinely included as part of the learning experience. In other disciplines, the same assumption underlies assignments like papers, team problem solving, oral presentations, and the like. Such assignments are examples of students doing something rather than just hearing about it. That's at least one reason why faculty regard it as cheating if students buy their papers online or otherwise arrange for someone else to go through the experience of learning for them. That's so basic an understanding of the importance of learning from experience in academe that it is seldom even mentioned.

When learning from experience is mentioned, it's usually in the context of less traditional assignments and fields of learning such as service learning, fieldwork, internships, or studio arts. These are teaching situations in which faculty have less control over the learning experience than in the classroom, and in which they may not always be able to supervise their students at all times. The emphasis in such classes is on students developing skills that may seem to be only tangentially related to more traditional content knowledge and the critical thinking and research skills demonstrated in papers and tests. Unforeseen events are often the norm. Yet, faculty must still give feedback and grade students, often on criteria that are difficult to define and that often occur out of sight of the faculty member doing the grading. How can you develop a rubric for that?

The answer is, quite simply, the same way one develops every other rubric: through reflection and a step-by-step acknowledgment of what the professor wants her students to learn and how she can tell whether they have. One major difference is that learning from experience requires much the same sort of reflection and feedback from the students themselves and from external partners involved in the students' experiences. Rubrics (and assignments) created for that purpose must somehow take these factors into account.

None of that changes the fundamental nature of the rubric, however. In this chapter we look at how a rubric can be used to account for the needs of teaching and learning from experience. In the following four cases we show how rubrics can be designed to help students learn from experience:

- Hiroaki, a history professor, wanted his students to conduct original research in the National Archives.

- Maura, an art teacher, sought to convey the importance of process as well as product in development of the final art portfolio.

- Dimitri, a politics professor, refined his use of journals to capture what students learned while working with community political groups.

- Ali, a professor in University Studies, used a rubric for the senior seminar community-based learning project that specified norms for professional behavior in the workplace.

Learning From Experience for Traditional Assignments

Hiroaki, a history professor, assigned the following task for an upper-division class in modern American history:

> Using the online National Archives, find and print out 5 documents that you might use for a paper on how the Second Amendment has been interpreted over the years. Highlight what you see as the most important points in each document and the parts you might want to quote, and write a short (2- to 3-page) paper explaining why you think these points are particularly important. Be sure to include a thesis statement for this hypothetical paper.

In Hiroaki's mind, this assignment was preparatory in nature. The major assignment for the course was a term paper on a topic of the student's choosing. Hiroaki simply wanted to be sure his students knew how to navigate the National Archives, which he expected would or should be a major source of material for that final paper. He also hoped that asking for a thesis statement for a hypothetical paper might jump-start the students into thinking about the topic of their term paper.

The results were disappointing. No fewer than 7 students out of a class of 18 turned in documents that had been culled from secondary texts or other online sources. When faced with this fact and a failing grade, the students argued that they didn't see why it mattered where they found the documents, and asked that they be graded on the basis of their highlighting and explanations. Two felt they deserved extra credit for having sought out additional texts. Their arguments made it clear that they saw this as an exercise in critical analysis, not gathering data from original sources.

Hiroaki's objective, however, had been to have his students experience what it meant to do primary research in the National Archives. He thought that was obvious. It wasn't. He realized that the way he worded his assignment did not actually make that clear, and, since he did not use a rubric, the students had no other hints about what he wanted. The matter was eventually settled by having the students do another, similar assignment for a replacement grade, a compromise that enabled students to practice what he had not clearly conveyed in the beginning.

The following year, Hiroaki redid his assignment and added a rubric using the basic four-stage method: reflecting, listing, grouping and labeling, and application.

In his reflections, the first stage, Hiroaki spelled out his aims. His intent had been

1. to introduce his students to the online National Archives and have them navigate its waters on their own;

2. to have his students understand how many documents there were on any given topic and make their own determination of which were truly significant and which were not;

3. to understand how the thesis affects making such choices; and

4. to jump-start their thinking about possible topics for the term paper.

Last but not least, he wanted to know how well they had succeeded before they moved on to the more ambitious term paper.

On that last point in listing, the second stage, he focused on what the best student paper would look like. His lists included items such as:

- ✓ Did at least 5 keyword searches.
- ✓ Made sure the key words work well with the thesis.
- ✓ Used at least 3 links.
- ✓ Wrote a clear and well-developed thesis statement.
- ✓ Found at least 10 documents *relevant* to thesis statement.
- ✓ Clearly and fully described the search and elaborated on difficulties encountered and how the students overcame them.

His lists also included some of the analytical concerns evident in the original assignment. He still wanted his students to show some level of understanding of the historical context and broader implications of their topic, but those concerns were clearly outnumbered by more "nuts and bolts" demands for specific actions and problem-solving activities that a researcher would use when working with archives.

That was even more apparent when it came to grouping and labeling, the third stage of rubric creation. After sorting all of the items in the list into groups, he came up with three basic groups. The first, which he labeled "research," consisted mostly of items related to the process of using the site. The second, which he labeled "content," spelled out the number of documents he expected them to find and what he wanted to see included in the final package. Only the third, which he labeled "analysis," related to critical thinking about the subject at hand: that hypothetical thesis statement. As a final touch, he changed the title of the assignment that appeared at the top of the rubric from "The National Archives Experience Project" to the more prosaic, but infinitely clearer "Doing Research in the National Archives." (See Appendix A for a guidelines for writing a clear task description.)

The new rubric and task description were far more successful (Figure 8.1), and most students performed very well indeed. Including an entire dimension labeled "Research," along with corresponding

Doing Research in the National Archives

Task Description: Using the online National Archives, find and print out 5 documents that you might use for a paper on how the Second Amendment has been interpreted over the years. Highlight what you see as the most important points in each document, the parts you might want to quote. Then, write a short (500–700 words) paper explaining why you made the choices you did and why you rejected other possibilities. Discuss any difficulties you had in navigating the site, finding documents, and/or making your selections. Be sure to include a thesis statement for this hypothetical paper and justify your choices of documents and possible quotations in the context of that thesis statement.

	Excellent	Good	Needs Work
R E S E A R C H	• Documents are carefully selected for relevance to thesis, and paper discusses how and why at least 5 other options were rejected. • Paper includes a full description of how the documents were found, including links and key words used, difficulties encountered, and the rationale behind the final selection. • The search used at least 5 different, relevant key words and 2 relevant links. • Documents are clearly and fully identified and cited.	• Most of the documents selected are relevant, and the paper discusses how and why at least 3 other options were rejected. • Paper describes most of the links and key words used, difficulties encountered, and the rationale behind the final selection. • The search used at least 3 different, relevant key words and 1 relevant link. • Documents are clearly identified and cited.	• The relevance of the documents to the thesis is unclear, and the paper does not clarify this. There is little or no discussion of rejected options. • Paper describes few if any links and key words used, fails to recognize difficulties, and contains no clear rationale for finals selection. • Search used 2 or fewer key words and none of the links. • Documents are not clearly identified or cited.
C O N T E N T	• Paper is 500–700 words in length. • Paper is directly related to the documents attached. • Paper contains a clearly identified thesis statement. • Contains 5 complete documents that are directly relevant to the thesis statement. • Documents are printouts from the National Archives site.	• Paper is 400–800 words in length. • Paper mostly addresses the documents attached. • Paper reveals a thesis clearly enough to tell whether documents chosen are relevant. • Contains 5 complete documents that are mostly relevant to thesis. • Documents are printouts from the National Archives site.	• Contains a paper that is fewer than 400 words or more than 800 words. • Paper is only tangentially related or not related at all to documents attached. • Thesis is not clear in the paper. • Contains fewer or more than 5 documents and/or documents that are not relevant to thesis. • Documents are from somewhere other than the National Archives site.
A N A L Y S I S	• Thesis statement shows full awareness of the broader implications and context of the topic. • Highlighted points are well chosen and relevant to the position taken in the thesis statement. • Paper shows a full awareness of how documentation, context, and ongoing discoveries led to, changed, or reinforced the creation of a solid thesis statement.	• Thesis statement shows some awareness of the broader implications and context of the topic. • Highlighted points are mostly relevant to the position taken in the thesis statement. • Paper shows some awareness of how documentation, context, and ongoing discoveries led to, changed, or reinforced the creation of a solid thesis statement.	• The thesis statement shows no awareness of the broader implications and context of the topic, or there is no thesis statement. • Highlighted points seem random or are nonexistent. • Paper shows little or no understanding of how documentation, context, and ongoing discoveries led to, changed, or reinforced the creation of a solid thesis statement.

Figure 8.1 Hiroaki's rubric for doing research in the National Archives.

descriptions, made it clear that the process (the experience) of doing basic archival research was as important in this case as the product. The repeated references to a thesis and thesis statement, and the connection of that thesis to relevance and document selection, likewise reinforced the emphasis on how to direct what they learned from the experience of using the National Archives as historians. This was the original research experience he wanted them to have.

Rubrics for Classroom/Lab/Studio Behaviors

Lack of what some faculty deem appropriate behavior and dress on most college campuses is a bit like the weather: many complain about it but no one does anything about it. Almost no one. Some professional schools seek to communicate these standards regarding appropriate behavior and dress to help students learn and practice workplace norms. In addition, hands-on classes like labs and art studios often grade on behaviors and process as much as content knowledge in an effort to tell students how to behave in a professional setting as well.

That approach is exemplified in the lab rubric (see Figure 8.2). It takes some account of results in the form of lab reports to be handed in at the end of the lab session, but more of the rubric relates to process (how the experiment is designed and conducted) and behaviors, including basic civility, tidiness, and, of course, safety.

That emphasis is even more pronounced in an art studio rubric Maura created for an introductory class in studio art. This rubric and the decision to add a separate "Studio Utilization" grade at all came about almost accidentally, as a result of Maura's reflections while working on a rubric for final portfolios. As she considered what she wanted to see in a good portfolio, she realized that she was also thinking of students whose portfolios would definitely not be in the highest category, but who had worked hard, made the most of their studio art experience, and gained from that experience. Some of these students had also been those who helped the most in the studio, not just with materials, but with encouraging and supporting other students.

As she began reflecting and listing her highest expectations for a good portfolio, she realized that her criteria mostly ignored the value

Rubric for Conducting an Experiment in the Lab

Task Description: Conduct the assigned lab using the procedures and methods described in the following rubric. Turn in your laboratory report at the beginning of the next class period.

	Exemplary	Competent	Needs Work
Materials	All needed materials are present and entered on the lab report. The materials are appropriate for the procedure. The student is not wasteful of the materials.	All needed materials are present, but not all are entered on the lab report, or some materials are absent and must be obtained during the procedure. The materials are appropriate for the procedure.	All needed materials are not present and are not entered on the lab report. The materials are not all appropriate for the procedure and/or there are some major omissions.
Procedure	The procedure is well-designed and allows control of all variables selected. All stages of the procedure are entered on the lab report.	The procedure could be designed more efficiently, but it allows control of all variables selected. Most stages of the procedure are entered on the lab report.	The procedure does not allow control of all variables selected. Many stages of the procedure are not entered on the lab report.
Courtesy and safety	While conducting the procedure, the student is tidy, respectful of others, mindful of safety, and leaves the area clean.	While conducting the procedure, the student is mostly tidy, sometimes respectful of others, sometimes mindful of safety, and leaves the area clean only after being reminded.	While conducting the procedure, the student is untidy, not respectful of others, not mindful of safety, and leaves the area messy even after being reminded.
Purpose	Research question and hypothesis are stated clearly, and the relationship between the two is clear. The variables are selected.	Research question and hypothesis are stated, but one or both are not as clear as they might be, and/or the relationship between the two is unclear. The variables are selected.	Research question and hypothesis are not stated clearly, and the relationship between the two is unclear or absent. The variables are not selected.
Data collection	Raw data, including units, are recorded in a way that is appropriate and clear. The title of the data table is included.	Raw data, including units, are recorded, although not as clearly or appropriately as they might be. The title of the data table is included.	Raw data, including units, are not recorded appropriately and clearly. The title of the data table is not included.
Data analysis	Data are presented in ways (charts, tables, graphs) that best facilitate understanding and interpretation. Error analysis is included.	Data are presented in ways (charts, tables, graphs) that can be understood and interpreted, although not as clearly as they might be. Error analysis is included.	Date (chart tables, graphs) are not presented clearly. Error analysis is not included.
Evaluation of experiment	The results are fully interpreted and compared with literature values. The limitations and weaknesses are discussed, and suggestions are made about how to limit or eliminate them.	The results are interpreted and compared with literature values, but not as fully as they might be. The limitations and weaknesses are discussed, but few or no suggestions are made about how to limit or eliminate them.	The results are not interpreted in a logical way or compared with literature values. The limitations and weaknesses are not discussed, nor are suggestions made about how to limit or eliminate them.

Figure 8.2   Rubric for conducting an experiment in a laboratory.

of additional personal learning and interpersonal skills. She had included a dimension specifying that the work should show improvement over the semester and reflect the variety of styles, media, and principles of art that were introduced in class, but otherwise the focus was on the quality of the work and the comparative abilities of the students.

Yet, when she came to list her descriptions of an exemplary performance on a final portfolio rubric, she found that she was including such things as:

✓ Behaves courteously

✓ Helps others

✓ Tries everything at least once

✓ Makes a sincere effort

She also found herself thinking of one or two of her highly talented students who possessed very few of these traits. She wanted them especially to know that their talent was real and valuable, but she wanted them to receive feedback on these essential professional interpersonal and cooperative learning skills so they would be better able to work with their peers and progress in their artistic development.

As a result of those deliberations, Maura created her Studio Utilization rubric (Figure 8.3), which she handed out on the first day of class. She was surprised by the response. Many of her new students looked noticeably relieved and participated more fully in the class right from the start. Those students who had arrived with well-worn portfolios and art equipment ready, those who already considered themselves artists, were more resistant to the feedback on these interpersonal skills on the rubric at first, feeling that their talent and results should count for more than these interpersonal interactions. Most of them came around eventually and felt they had learned from the experience of getting specific feedback on their interpersonal skills in the studio.

But the happiest part of Maura's experiment with her new rubric was her retention rate. Usually at least two or three students dropped the class in the first few weeks. However, she lost no students during the entire term she implemented her Studio Utilization rubric, and

Studio Art: Studio Utilization

Students are expected to attend all studio sessions, be on time, and participate actively when present. Participation includes working on assigned projects when in the studio, helping to set out the materials and clean up afterward, and interacting with other students in an appropriate manner to further everyone's improvement. Because this is a hands-on class, no more than 3 absences are permitted. Students who miss more than 3 sessions without a documented reason will receive an F. Those who miss more than 3 sessions with an acceptable, documented reason will be permitted to drop the class with no record.

The instructor realizes that talents and experience vary. A willingness to experiment and to do one's best on all projects is important. This grade recognizes perseverance and sincerity of effort regardless of the results.

	Master	Craftsman	Apprentice
Attendance	Student missed no more than one studio class. Student always arrived on time and did not leave early.	Student missed no more than two studio classes. Student was late or left early no more than twice.	Student missed 3 or more studio classes. If documented = W; if not documented = F.
Behavior	Student always helped set out and clean up materials in a thoughtful, efficient manner.	Student helped set out and clean up materials most of the time. Efforts may not always have been efficient.	Student did not help set out or clean up materials and/or did so in a disruptive fashion.
Interactions	Student was courteous in relating to others in the studio and showed leadership in helping out.	Student was courteous in relating to others but showed little if any leadership.	Student was sometimes rude to others and disruptive in ways that made it difficult for others to work.
Creativity	Student experimented with all media, styles, and principles of art introduced by the instructor, and made a sincere effort to incorporate new knowledge in personal work.	Student experimented with most of the media, styles, and principles of art introduced by the instructor, but did not always connect these in a meaningful way to personal work.	Student refused to experiment with new media, styles, and principles of art on several occasions and/or did such experiments in a dismissive, slapdash manner.
Perseverance	Student finished all 5 assigned projects in a polished fashion. When faced with difficulties, student made every effort to overcome them before giving up or giving in to frustration in the studio.	Student turned in all 5 assigned projects, but some were unpolished and/or unfinished. When faced with difficulties, student made a serious effort to overcome them before giving up and/or giving in to frustration.	Student did not turn in all 5 assigned projects. When faced with difficulties, student generally gave up easily and/or reacted in a seriously disruptive fashion in the studio.

Figure 8.3 Maura's art studio utilization rubric.

while she still has the occasional student who bails out early, her rate remains consistently low. Students who had good interpersonal skills felt more valued and more aware of the value of what they were learning in the art studio.

Rubrics for Service Learning

Assessing students in the classroom is hard enough, but at least when they're there, we can see them. What do we do when we can't see them, when the work we want them to do mostly takes place away from our oversight? That happens on field trips, internships, study abroad, research projects, and, above all, in service learning or, as some call it, community-based learning. That was the concern of Dimitri, a professor teaching an American politics course in which he asked his students to participate in some sort of political action group while at the same time doing more traditional research about that action group. To enhance that learning experience and to enable him to monitor and grade it, he asked his students to keep a weekly journal.

Dimitri loved the idea of including this learning from a real political experience in what was otherwise a fairly conventional political science class. In their evaluations, students regularly mentioned it as the highlight of the class, and he saw this as a way to emphasize not just how the system worked, but also to promote the idea that this sort of activity was part and parcel of the duties of being an American citizen.

He did have a few doubts about the value of journaling, however. He himself did not keep a journal. He accepted colleagues' statements regarding the possibilities for personal growth that journaling offered, but he was aware that he rarely saw much evidence of this in the student journals he received. He also couldn't think of any other way to document and grade the community-based learning assignment, short of following each student around individually. Unwilling to give up on the assignment, he decided to rethink the whole participation and journal assignment to see if he could fix it.

He began by listing his past disappointments when he assigned journal keeping in the past:

✓ Some journals are handwritten, which is fine if the students have legible handwriting, but what about those whose writing I cannot read?

✓ Many of the journals don't seem to have been maintained consistently; I suspected that many students produce them the night before they are due, adding plausible dates to each entry. But the end product doesn't show growth over time, which is one purpose of this assignment.

✓ Students often don't comment on their ongoing research, readings, or classes or, if they do, they don't connect these to the activities they document in the field despite the fact that I state this clearly in the syllabus and the task assignment, and remind them in class.

✓ Students even more frequently don't make connections between their own feelings/lives and their participatory experiences, although that's also in the syllabus, accompanied by frequent class reminders.

✓ Conversely, some students often mistake their journal for a diary and include personal information and commentary that is not connected at all to the class or the political group they are studying, at least not in any way I can determine.

✓ Students don't take advantage of the handwritten journaling format to add samples of their activities or creative or other unconventional touches that might showcase their own talents and offer unexpected insights.

✓ Journals take too long to read and grade.

As he looked over his list, Dimitri found that, except for the last point, all of his concerns highlighted the strengths of journaling when it was done correctly. His concern was simply that the students weren't doing what he hoped they would do with their journals.

The solution to these problems came to him in the form of a borrowed rubric designed for a class in advanced educational psychology that included no community outreach component but had a journal-keeping assignment. This rubric proved surprisingly easy to adapt because students essentially graded their own work through a reflection on their written field notes, a reflection on reflections. The educational psychology teacher called it a "metareflection." His rubric looked like Figure 8.4.

The students photocopied relevant portions of their journals and wrote this metareflection (described more fully in Stevens & Cooper, 2009). The metareflection assignment and rubric were a success. Dimitri found that grading these reflections was relatively quick and easy. Better yet, the quality of the students' commentary on their experience had markedly improved, and he learned how they regarded their work in the field site. And he wasn't toting a hefty box of journals back and forth from his office.

He had one remaining concern, however. He suspected that a few of the students may have worked hard on the metareflections for the two entries they turned in, but otherwise he wondered whether they had really done the journaling. Not doing the journaling defeated the point of the assignment and didn't seem fair to the other students. But what could he do to add a bit of accountability to the assignment without significantly increasing his workload again?

The next year, he used the same assignment and rubric but added one final requirement: a mid-semester call for the full journals to be turned in so he could see whether the students were keeping them up. He had no intention of giving them anything more than a cursory read. Instead, he made himself a little checklist (Figure 8.5), a very simple scoring guide rubric enabling him to check off whether the journals fulfilled the assignment.

His checklist was initially based on his earlier concerns, but he crossed out criteria that he realized the metareflection rubric already addressed. He dispensed with his stricture about students using their journals as diaries; after all he was not reading the whole journal, just scanning it quickly. He did not care whether they included extraneous personal information because he was not going to read every page. Only the ones they selected as relevant entries on which to write their metareflection. Provided those weren't the two entries selected for the metareflections, he reasoned, there was no harm, and some possible benefit, for the students themselves in including that incidental, more diary-like material. In the process he solved his concern about illegible handwriting. He required that the metareflections, like all essays, be

Metareflections on Journal Entries, 10 points

Task description: Keep a journal to collect your thoughts, questions, understandings, notes, and information related to your field project. As a citizen, if not as a political professional, you develop your ability to handle the complexity of your views and duties through reflection. A journal is a well-documented way to develop your reflective capacity. You will use the journal to chronicle your field activities, make connections between your field actions/activities and classroom experiences/research, and reflect on your emotional and other personal responses to your field experiences.

At the end of the term you will write two metareflections. Select, scan, or photograph two journal entries that you consider to be the most significant, and write a metareflection on each entry. Each metareflection should be at least one page and may include quotations from your journal. Address how this entry affected your thinking, addressed a problem, or surprised you.

Dimension	Description	Pts.	Comment
Table of contents	Submit a photocopy or .jpeg scan of table of contents in your journal. Format for table of contents: Date/Entry description/ Page Number(s)	2	
Entries	Submit photocopies or .jpeg scan of the two significant journal entries you have chosen to reflect upon.	2	
Metareflections	Write a 1-page "metareflection" on each journal entry. That is 2 (two) metareflections that: **Reflection #1 (check all that apply): TITLE:** _____ • Includes a synopsis of the events and activities of the week the entry was based on. • Describes the implications of the entry for you as a citizen and/or political professional. • Makes connections between your field actions/activities and classroom experiences and research. • Reflects on your emotional and other personal responses to your field experiences. • Elaborates on what the entry means for you in the future. • Compares and contrasts your thinking from the beginning of the term to the end of the term. • Other topic that this entry addresses: _____ **Reflection #2 (check all that apply): TITLE:** _____ • Includes a synopsis of the events and activities of the week the entry was based on. • Describes the implications of the entry for you as a citizen and/or political professional. • Makes connections between your field actions/activities and classroom experiences and research. • Reflects on your emotional and other personal responses to your field experiences. • Elaborates on what the entry means for you in the future. • Compares and contrasts your thinking from the beginning of the term to the end of the term. • Other topic that this entry addresses: _____	6	
Creativity	Scan (or photograph and upload as a .jpeg) anything you would call a creative enhancement that you have added to your journal.	2	Bonus Points

Figure 8.4 Dimitri's rubric for metareflection on journal entries.

Mid-Semester Journal Checklist

Student Name: _____

Note: This checklist is intended purely as feedback. It is not a grading guide, but it does contain the criteria on which you will be graded when you turn in the final journal. If you think I have overlooked something you did, please ask me about it.

- Journal was turned in on time.
- There is one dated entry for each week of class.
- Each entry is at least one page long.
- Pages are numbered.
- There is a *table of contents* for the journal entries with date, title, and page number.
- ~~Journal is legible and easy to read.~~
- ~~Journal chronicles actions/activities undertaken, at least one per week.~~
- ~~Entries connect actions/activities to ongoing research, readings, and classes.~~
- ~~Entries reference emotional and personal responses that relate to actions/ activities.~~
- Journal includes brochures, documents, charts, artwork, and other examples of the work undertaken in day-to-day actions/activities referenced.
- Journal includes other creative touches such as photos, art work, or creative writing that add unexpected insights into the actions/activities referenced.
- ~~Entries stick to the topic and do not include large amounts of irrelevant information.~~

Figure 8.5   Dimitri's mid-semester journal checklist showing the original version and what was eliminated before the list was presented to the students.

typed, and using them as a guide, he thought he would be able to decipher text referred to in the original entries that had been photocopied.

That left only one of his original concerns. When he collected the journals mid-semester for a quick scan to ensure that students were actually keeping the journal, he would still be hefting a heavy box of journals down the hall. On the advice of a colleague, he purchased a plastic rolling cart.

Rubrics With Community-Based Partners

Ali, a professor teaching a senior capstone class that included a community outreach component, found a different way to evaluate what his students were doing. Unable to be on-site all the time, he simply asked those who were there. In his capstone class, students worked with at-risk kids in a community art center, but the students worked different hours and often with different staff members.

Initially, in consultation with the partner institution, Ali decided that the staff member at the site would only need to document that the student showed up. Then both sides realized this was an opportunity to tell students about some of the expectations of professionals in this setting. Together they developed a simple checklist (Figure 8.6) that would do three things: include the expectations of the art center, give Ali a way to assess student engagement at the site, and, most important, alert both students and staff members to what both he and the center staff expected of them. Because the staff were busy at the site, they made the rubric fairly easy to use and yet as specific as they could by using a variation on a scoring guide rubric.

Ali's inclusion of appropriate dress and professional attitude in the rubric attracted the attention of Ellen, a business professor, who was in charge of overseeing interns. Ali was surprised when she asked to borrow and adapt his rubric, and pointed out that his definition of "appropriate" and "professional" related to maintaining the respect and attention of 5-year-olds with paintbrushes in their hands. Ellen pointed out that since the rubric was designed to be filled in by professionals who understand what constitutes "appropriate" and "professional" in their fields, she would have to do very little to adapt it to a corporate environment. All she wanted was an easy form that would guide on-site observers in providing basic feedback. She made almost no changes to the rubric except to add one more dimension, which she labeled "Potential." It asked the question, "If you had a position available, would you consider hiring this student?" The original professor, Ali, eventually added that to his rubric, too. In both cases, students received the rubric ahead of time and were given a copy of the rubric with feedback at the end of the term.

Conclusion

Most faculty members include some form of learning from experience in their classes, whether it is cast in a traditional mode such as the National Archives project or involves full-scale community outreach programs. Many struggle with how to give students feedback on their learning from experience. Used as grading guides and teaching tools, rubrics can help enormously to make experiential learning easier and more rewarding for all concerned. In the history class, we illustrated

Feedback for Community Arts Student Participants

Student Name: _____   **Date:** _____

Dear Staff Member:

Thank you for welcoming our students into your program. This experience is an essential part of their preparation for becoming socially responsible citizens.

We would appreciate it if those of you who have had contact with our Community Outreach students could comment on your impressions of their participation in your program. Any other feedback you care to provide would also be most welcome. We will share your comments with the students, but we ask that you include your name anonymously so we can contact you if we have further questions.

Staff name: _____

	Criteria	Yes/No (please circle one)	Comments and Explanations
Attendance	Did the student show up on time?	Yes No	
	If there were excusable absences, did the student call in?	Yes No	
Active learning	Did the student take full advantage of growth opportunities?	Yes No	
	Did the student ask for help or mentoring when needed?	Yes No	
Leadership	Did the student behave responsibly on the job?	Yes No	
	Did the student help?	Yes No	
	Were there any special incidents that indicate leadership potential?	Yes No	
Dress	Did the student dress appropriately for the setting?	Yes No	
Demeanor	Did the student behave professionally toward clients and coworkers?	Yes No	
Feedback	Did the student demonstrate good listening skills when learning about professional behavior/demeanor?'	Yes No	

Figure 8.6   Ali's rubric for student feedback from community arts partner.

how the addition of a rubric clarified what the professor expected in the field setting, the National Archives. The rubric served as a way to determine whether students could undertake research projects on their own. In the art class, the rubric allowed the professor to convey some of the tacit norms and interpersonal skills that are valued in an art community where peer feedback and support are essential. The journal-keeping activity in the politics class helped the professor encourage students to reflect on their learning from the experience of working with a community political organization. And in the capstone community outreach project, Ali found a way to ask for feedback from his partner institution without asking too much of already over-worked staff. In all of these different classes, rubrics were an effective way to emphasize and document learning from experience, especially in the following ways:

- Rubrics clarified what we expect students to do in field settings.
- Rubrics conveyed some valued professional norms and interpersonal skills that are often taken for granted.
- Rubrics included practicing reflective writing (and reflection in general) in a journal to learn from experience.

9

RUBRICS AND ONLINE LEARNING

Student faces. The faces of our students. Some faculty members take pictures, but even those of us who don't have a photo album in our minds of students past and present, the best and the most challenging, the funny and the serious, and some we simply remember for no clear reason. Until recently, we've taken it for granted that face-to-face communication is an intrinsic part of teaching. Sure, there were correspondence courses, but few faculty members participated in these, and fewer yet thought they were an adequate replacement for actual classrooms. Then came the Internet and online learning, and all bets were off.

Online learning offers immediacy and a possibility for personal feedback that comes close to what is possible in classroom learning, but there is no doubt that, even with Skype and videoconferencing, the face-to-face aspect of teaching is seriously limited if not actually gone. That's important. In face-to-face classroom settings, teaching faculty members have an array of activities that ensure good communication. During lectures, the professor can note all the subtle cues that indicate that students are not attending and can quickly adjust to boost attention. Even faculty members who manage to generate discussion groups online among students through forums, listservs, or even Skype or videoconferencing, cannot keep track of interchanges and responses the way they could if they were all seated around a table or at circled desks.

Online teaching also affects how faculty members relate to students outside class. Skype, if available to both parties, can allow some degree of face-to-face interaction during office hours so the professor can respond directly and often immediately to individual needs, but Skype obviously doesn't permit us to offer a student a cup of coffee, or take her for a walk around the quad, or hand him a tissue when necessary. Those interactions are important. Kezar (2011) summarizes the positive effects of all this communication on student success: "Students who talk to their professors, attend office hours, and engage with faculty outside of class tend to persist, graduate and do better in school" (para. 1). Faculty who listen to students in and out of class, encourage attendance at office hours, and talk to students outside class have a powerful impact on student success. So it is not just what we do during class time that counts. How can we do this in online learning?

Even though rubrics cannot solve all or even most of the challenges posed by the emerging world of online teaching, they can be a powerful tool in making the online learning experience rewarding for all concerned. Rubrics are an essential element in fostering positive communication. With rubrics, students can trust that the professor has consistent grading standards. Students can read the grading criteria, see the specific levels of performance of the assignments, and gauge their effort accordingly. Using rubrics in the online classroom is one of several ways to create a "sense of presence" for faculty and students alike that approximates the real sense of presence in face-to-face instruction.

This chapter describes how rubrics can be developed and used in the online classroom. Through a case study, we show how one faculty member, Serap, designed new rubrics for three typical online learning activities. These student activities and assignments were:

- Participation in an online discussion forum
- Creation of a wiki page for group work online
- Peer review of a fellow student's final project

In addition, we include a section on the "nuts and bolts" of rubric management online, offering several ways to get rubrics in students' hands and to give them feedback on the rubric. We conclude with some thoughts on how rubrics contribute to a "sense of presence" in online instruction, one of the essential criteria for a successful online class (Capsi & Blau, 2008; Lehman & Conceição, 2010).

Rubric for Participating in an Online Discussion Forum

Serap, an assistant professor of sociology in her third year, was asked by her department chair to convert her successful senior-level seminar class, "Writing in Your Profession," to an online format. After three years of developing and teaching this class, the chair felt that Serap had really figured out the best way to teach it. Yet, Serap did not know how to make it work in an online environment. Since she had her course objectives, which should not change, she thought she was off to a good start.

She realized that she needed to reflect on some of the activities she depended on in the face-to-face setting and to determine whether they would work at all online. She made a chart of the various activities she had found to be effective in the classroom to see whether there were any online equivalents that would help her accomplish the same objectives and give her some new ideas about different ways to deliver content. She created the chart shown in Figure 9.1, and, as she continued to think about face-to-face versus online class activities and assignments, the chart began to take shape and fill in.

First was the problem of delivering the content of the course. One thing she feared was that she would not have the advantage of class discussions to find out day by day what her students knew, how engaged they were, and what questions they had. She had previously devoted about half of her face-to-face class to lecture, with the other half divided between class discussion and small-group work on written and oral projects. She thought to herself, "Lecture, hmm . . . how do I do that online?" She checked into the possibility of using some form of videoconferencing only to discover that this option was not available at her university. She also considered videotaping her lectures, but after looking into the matter, she decided that for her first foray into teaching online just appropriately transforming the content for online learning was challenge enough. She decided to focus her efforts on finding a simpler online alternative for delivering the content and making sure that her students were getting it. Figure 9.1 shows how Serap tried to match her current face-to-face course activities and assignments with online equivalents. It also indicates what kind of rubrics she might need to assess students in this new learning environment.

Student activities and assignments for my course, Writing in Your Profession.
Students will create a project for use in their professional life (newsletter, brochure, blog, or website).

Course Objective	Course activities and assignments related to the objective				
	Text readings	Class discussion	Group work	Term paper	Culminating project
Activities used in face-to-face course	Read text about developing a project for their specific audience.	Discuss issues in class related to project development.	Worked together on class presentation on analysis of survey data designed for my audience.	Write short paper summarizing results from survey of audience.	Submit final project using survey data to revise and refine final project.
Activities adapted to an online format	Online discussion forum with questions on readings		Drop this for this first year.	Keep this; just submit online.	Keep this; just submit online.
Rubrics needed	Make rubric for quantity and quality of responses to the forum.			Use same rubric from face-to-face class.	Use same rubric as used for face-to-face class.

Figure 9.1 Serap's chart with overall course objectives comparing class activities, face-to-face and online, Year 1.

She shifted her focus away from lectures and turned her attention instead to discussions as her chief means of ensuring that students actively engaged with the material and whether they were learning what she was teaching. She talked to a colleague, Paulina, who used online forums extensively in her traditional teaching.

"Students use the online discussion forum much like a face-to-face class discussion," Paulina told Serap, "but the discussion is different online. Online students won't all be there at the same time for anything. Students post their answers to a discussion prompt in the forum about the course readings in their own time. Others, including you, the instructor, read their answers and respond whenever you want."

"It seems to me that to make this transition to online successful, I could use the discussion forum to make sure students are thinking about and learning the content even if they cannot be there at the same time," Serap mused.

Actually Serap's research had already confirmed that, after e-mail, the online discussion forum is the most commonly used teaching activity online (Kearsley, 2000). Now, Paulina, who taught regularly online, was also recommending that method.

"There are some other advantages to using forums," Paulina added. "Unlike face-to-face class discussions, no one can 'hide out' in the back rows of the classroom. And, you know, Serap, I have also seen students spontaneously offer assistance to each other online as well as post their expected reflections on the content. Surprised me at first that this was possible online; I thought they would only answer the questions asked!"

All of this feedback persuaded Serap that she was on the right track in focusing on online discussion to cover lecture content, but she wondered what should be on the final rubric for the discussion forum. She had never used a rubric for participation when teaching in the classroom. But, then, as she reflected on what a typical classroom discussion was like, especially one where the students participated fully in the discussion, there were still always the issues of who talks, how much, and how well.

"I want to design a rubric for online discussion. I think there are both quantity and quality issues," Serap told Paulina. "On the one hand, there is the question of how often students respond not only to me, but also to their peers. On the other hand, there is the question of how well they are responding and thinking about the discussion prompt, the quality issue. How can I capture both of those on a rubric?"

Paulina told her that the quantity issue could be solved quite easily. "One thing about computers and online course management systems is that they can count and report out. The system can count how often students have responded to your prompt in the discussion forum and even how often the students have responded to each other. This makes online instruction different from face-to-face. You can track student participation. This helps with the quantity issue. You cannot do that in the give-and-take of face-to-face classroom discussion."

"The quality issue is the other side of the discussion forum assessment coin," Serap continued. "The forum should be a place where my students can struggle with some central themes of the course and reflect and contribute their own points of view. A rubric is a simple and direct way to give students some guidelines about how to contribute in the forum when discussing course content and applying the content to their own life experience."

To deal with that concern, Serap created a rubric for her online discussion forum. The rubric Serap initially created for discussion forum contained only three dimensions, "Content," "Application to experience," and "Writing conventions." As she was writing the descriptions of these dimensions on the rubric, however, she realized that there was more to quality of response than these three dimensions. There was also the matter of courtesy and respect.

"Paulina, what about the quality of the relationships students establish among themselves online through these discussions?" Serap asked. "Because students are interacting with one another, they should feel they are not alone in the class and can build relationships with one another. But online communication is a bit more distant than face-to-face. Tone and facial expressions are gone and that leads to misunderstandings. Also, it's just plain easier to be careless in your communication online like on email and not imagine the effect of your response on someone you've never seen. Should I be worried that they might say something even hurtful or inappropriate in their responses?"

"Yes," Paulina agreed. "I worry about it in face-to-face teaching, too, but online can be worse. Of course, we want students to be respectful of different opinions and not hurt other students with their comments. I put this on my rubrics as a 'Response to others' dimension to show that I will be paying attention to how they treat each other online, just like I would in a face-to-face classroom."

Serap added a fourth dimension to her rubric, one in which she detailed how she expected her students to treat one another. Figure 9.2 is the final rubric she created with all the dimensions on it.

Rubric for Creating a Wiki Page for Online Group Work

During her first term teaching online, Serap had used readings, the discussion forum with its rubric, and two writing assignments. She was satisfied with what the students learned and the final projects they produced. The discussion forum worked well. The rubric set them up for success. For her second term of online teaching she decided to expand the number of student activities. She thought it would be good to get the students working together to learn how to find some of their own online resources and share them with each other, thereby taking full advantage of the opportunities the Internet offered. She went back to Paulina.

"Great idea!" Paulina responded. "I do it all the time. I have my students work in groups to create a wiki page that contains documents and websites that other students can use as resources for their final term paper."

"I've heard of wikis," Serap replied, "but I'm not sure I even know exactly what a wiki is."

Paulina jumped right in, "A wiki is a collaborative website you set up where students can add their own pages with resources, files and links to websites. The ongoing research for the final project becomes truly a collaborative project."

"Sounds great," said Serap, "but will they know how to do that? I don't."

"There's a YouTube video, http://youtu.be/-dnL00TdmLY, that will show them how wikis work and how they can edit pages themselves. You might want to look at it, too, before you create the assignment," Paulina explained.

Serap watched the YouTube video and was surprised to find out how easy it was to create a wiki. Indeed, that very day, she went to

Online Discussion Forum Rubric

Task Description: Each student is expected to participate weekly in the online discussion forum. Participation means:

- Address the weekly question on the discussion forum submitted by the instructor.
- Respond to at least two other discussion forum posts that other students have made.

Since I am still grappling with the expectations of the online discussion, I have created a rubric that will allow me to give you feedback on the quantity and quality of posts you have entered. Remember, even though we do not have an opportunity for face-to-face discussion, it is still important for me to know how well you understand the content of the course. I am also interested in helping you get to know each other as you would in a face-to-face class. Therefore, not only is your initial response to the teacher-posed question important, but so are your responses to your peers' posts.

Dimension	Exemplary = 3 points	Competent = 2 points	Needs improvement = 1 – 0 points	Score
Content	Accurate citation of facts and ideas. Consistently integrates ideas across readings, identifying bigger themes.	Mostly accurate citing of facts and ideas from the readings. Integrates ideas a few times.	No attention to accurate citing. Does not integrate or attempt to see how chapter ideas are connected under larger themes.	
Application to experience	Describes several ways the content is relevant to personal life and experiences.	States the content is relevant to past experience but does not show how specifically.	Does not address how the content is relevant to prior experience.	
Response to others	Responds much more than twice a week. Offers constructive, helpful, supportive comments to others. Respectful of opinions that are different from their own.	Responds twice a week to other students. Reiterates what other students have said without being especially helpful or supportive. Respectful of opinions that are different from their own.	Does not respond to other students' posts. Not respectful (0 points).	
Writing conventions	Clarity of expression.	Mostly understandable writing.	Too many colloquialisms or grammar mistakes that affect clarity. Many misspellings.	

Figure 9.2   Serap's rubric for online discussion forum.

www.wikispaces.com and created a wiki for her class. The next day, she showed it to Paulina.

"I'm using the wiki to replace the old group project I had when I taught this class face-to-face," she told Paulina. "In the past I would divide the students into groups according to which type of final project they will be creating: brochure, newsletter, or blog. For the online class, each group will build a wiki page; it can be a page of resources for creating the final project, collaboratively designed."

"I think you'll be pleased with the results," said Paulina after she looked over Serap's chart and new wiki. "This is another place where online learning can be better than face-to-face, Serap. You know that problem we always have with groups, where students get frustrated because they feel that one person ends up doing all the work? That won't happen so much with the wiki version. There is a page, called 'Recent changes,' that tracks anything anyone does to any page on the wiki by date, name of the person, and what they did. You can track student involvement with the project every step of the way. Those who do the majority of the work will get full credit for it, and the others will know that if they slack off, you'll know and it will affect their grade."

Serap knew she would need a rubric to grade her new wiki, but realized that she would not have to create one from scratch. She had done group work before in this class and she had a rubric for that. Now, all she had to do was adapt it to the online project. Figure 9.3 is what she came up with to score the students' wiki resource page.

As she made her adaptations, she realized that she was adding considerably more explanation to her task description because she did not have the luxury of face-to-face explanations. Words, she realized, were one of the big differences between teaching online and teaching face-to-face. More words were necessary to ensure that students could follow the steps and collaboratively design the wiki the way she wanted.

Rubric for Peer Review of a Draft Version of a Final Project

Paulina also suggested another way students could interact online and learn from each other. "I have the students work in pairs and give each other feedback on the rough drafts of their writing," she told Serap.

Group Project   Scoring Guide Rubric

Task Description: In groups of 3, you are to collaborate with each other to create a wiki page. Each of you has chosen a project for this class: brochure, newsletter, blog, or website. The people in your group are doing the same type of project. While you are learning about creating this project and doing the other assignments for the class, collect references on why and how to do the project you have chosen. Then the three of you will work together to present these references to other students via a page on the course wiki. I have created a page for each group. Here are the steps I think you will need to complete.

1. Meet online and share e-mail addresses.
2. Gather references and citations about why and how to create your type of project. This means you will be looking for different ways to create, for example, a newsletter. You will be looking for articles and/or YouTube or TeacherTube videos you can use on the wiki page to inform others about how to do this type of project.
3. Learn how to post these on the wiki through the use of the "edit" and "save" buttons. Watch the video on the home page of the wiki, wikisinplainEnglish, which will clarify how wikis work and what the "edit" and "save" buttons mean.
4. Lay out the page so the reader can quickly see what you have learned and can access the links you have included.
5. This is a collaborative project. Collaboration counts. Work to include everyone's ideas.

Dimension	Description of an exemplary wiki page	Score/Comments
Content	Accurate information included Quotes from references are cited High level of understanding about how to do the project	10 pts.
Professional presentation: grammar, writing conventions	No grammatical errors Writing flows smoothly Citations follow APA formatting Quotations and other information are easy to understand Organized/logical presentation/professional tone Introduction engages the reader and enhances reader's motivation to continue reading	10 pts.
Professional presentation: Visual layout	Catches reader's attention through blocks of color and separation of textual elements Uses color Only 2 fonts	10 pts.
Creative enhancements	Engaging/eye-catching Clever use of color or materials or layout Different/unusual	5 pts.
Collaboration	Evident that everyone has contributed to the page "Discussion" tab on the wiki documents the interactions as the page is worked on Discussion is constructive and respectful	5 pts.

Figure 9.3   Serap's rubric for group creation of a wiki page.

"Peer reviewing?" Serap asked. "Yes, I used to have them do that in the classroom, but I'm not sure how to adapt it to the Internet. In class, I would just circulate as they were working together and make sure they were all on track. I can't do that online."

"That is a problem," Paulina agreed. "Unless you give them ongoing guidance, they tend to give vague, positive responses. I'm not sure whether they do that to be nice or just because it's easier or because they are unsure what to say, but you need to get through to them that positive unspecified feedback is not really helpful."

"How do you overcome that?" Serap asked.

"I give them a rubric that guides the kind of feedback they might give. It's pretty basic, a list of the kinds of things that are important to think about when giving feedback, and I grade them on their feedback. It seems to work."

Serap used Paulina's rubric as a model and adapted it to her own assignment, but she kept the three-step process Paulina recommended (see Figure 9.4):

1. She had the students review each other's work and put their comments on the rubric.

2. The students turned in the peer review feedback rubric filled in. Then she provided feedback to each reviewer on how well he or she had done in offering helpful feedback on a fellow student's work.

3. She sent the filled-out rubric on to the person whose work was being reviewed, adding her own comments and suggestions if she felt they were necessary.

When she was finished, Serap realized she needed to keep a record of the adaptations she had undertaken to put her teaching online. Such a chart not only would serve as a template for future adaptations, but it also would document what she had done, for both her own benefit and promotion and tenure purposes. Figure 9.5 shows how Serap charted what she had done in creating her online course.

"Nuts and Bolts" of Using Rubrics Online

Teaching online requires considerable adaptations. Even how you use rubrics changes. In face-to-face teaching, using a rubric seems

Peer Review Feedback Rubric for Student Project

Task Description: Your job is to review *drafts* of two other student projects. This form indicates some of the criteria that are important to review and provides a way to give feedback to your peer.

1. Review the draft version of your peer's final project. Enter your comments on the following form.
2. Turn in your comments for your peer to me. I will check off that you have done them.
3. I will then send them to the student.

Reviewer (you): _____ Date of review: _____

Type of student project you are reviewing (check one):
_____ Brochure   _____ Newsletter   _____ Blog

Student Name (peer): _____ E-mail: _____

URL (if blog) or file name if newsletter or brochure:

_____

Dimension	Exemplary product will have	As reviewer, my comments
1. Quality of the content	Relevant title Engaging content Text is easy to read. Links to other materials	
2. Layout of the project	Colorful layout Balance of text and images Uses only 2–3 font types	
3. Writing conventions	Correct grammar Correct punctuation Links that work	
4. Comments on the project as a whole. Note things that caught your attention, confused you, or that you would like to see more of.		

Figure 9.4   Serap's rubric for peer review of student projects.

relatively simple. The professor creates and presents the rubric using one of the models laid out in Chapter 4, and the students have it on hand while they do their work. When they turn in their papers, they attach the rubric to the assignment. The professor grades the

Student activities and assignments for my course, Writing in Your Profession.
Students will create a project for use in their professional life (newsletter, brochure, blog, or website).

Course Objective	Course activities and assignments related to the objective				
	Year 1			Year 2	
	Text readings	Class discussion	Group work	Term paper	Culminating project
How to use in face-to-face course	Read text about developing a project for my specific audience.	Discuss issues in class related to project development.	Work together on class presentation on analysis of survey data designed for my audience.	Write a short paper summarizing results from survey of audience.	Submit final project online, using survey data to revise and refine final product.
How to use in an online format	Online discussion forum questions on readings.	Divide into groups; make a wiki page together with resources on project topic.	Use the same assignment online.	Have students peer-review draft of final project.	
Rubrics I need to make	Make rubric for number and quality of responses to the forum.	Create rubric for creation of wiki page by groups.	Use old rubric from face-to-face class.	Rubric for peer-review process of student draft projects	

Figure 9.5 Serap's chart with objectives comparing activities, face-to-face and online, Years 1 and 2.

assignment with the rubric. Rubric and assignment are together. Online, it is a different story. To begin with, both the rubric and the student papers are in different computer files and students may not see them as connected. Here are several ways to link the rubric to the assignment:

1. **Linking the rubric to the assignment.** When students read about the assignment on the syllabus and/or in the "dropbox" or assignment description area in an online course management system, include a link to the rubric file for that particular assignment. That way they can download the rubric and read it as they do the assignment. This gets the rubric to the students and matches it with the assignment description.

2. **Giving feedback on the rubric.** Teach students how to attach the rubric to the last page of the assignment they are turning in. This is not complicated, but we have found that students don't find it intuitive. If it is appended to the assignment as the last page, it is easy for the professor to give feedback on the paper using Microsoft Word's Track Changes function, and then, at the end of the paper, there is the rubric to enter feedback. This is better than having students separately download the rubric and their papers from the course management system (often referred to as a CMS) like Desire-2Learn or Blackboard. This way the rubric is in the paper itself. All students have to do is download the rubric onto their desktop. Open it. "Select all." Copy. (Now it is in their compter's clipboard.) Open their paper. Go to the last page. From the dropdown menus, select "Insert new page." Click. Hit "Paste" (Command + V), and the computer will find the clipboard file where the rubric is located and with Command + V, will insert it as the last page on their paper.

These steps get the rubric in the same document as student work. After that, it is easy to read the student work using, for example, Track Changes, and when the professor gets to the last page, he or she can fill in the rubric.

Contribution of Rubrics to a "Sense of Presence" in Online Teaching

Serap's use of rubrics in her online teaching is an excellent demonstration of the power of rubrics in fostering communication online and

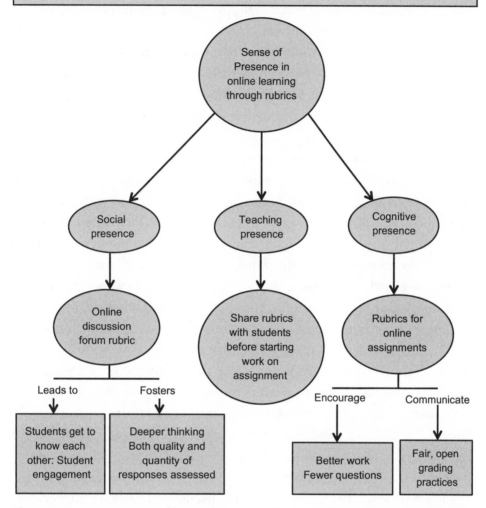

Figure 9.6 Concept map of how rubrics contribute to a "sense of presence" online.

creating a "sense of presence." Even though students are solely interacting with the instructor and other students in cyberspace, a "sense
of presence" in online instruction conveys the feeling that real people
are present. Some describe it as "being there" as a faculty member and
"being together" with other students (Lehman & Conceição, 2010,
p. 4).

There are three types of presence that help students feel like they
are in a real classroom: social presence, teaching presence, and cognitive presence (Lehman & Conceição, 2010). Figure 9.6 is a concept
map that illustrates the three different kinds of presence and how
rubrics support the development of each of these.

Social Presence

Social presence grows when faculty and students interact frequently online in a variety of contexts. A social presence is the feeling and knowledge that other students are together in the same class and the faculty member is also present. Rubrics assist in structuring faculty and student interactions. One of the main ways to structure communication online is through a discussion forum. Discussion forums mimic the structure of a dialogue in a social interaction, but students respond to a written faculty (or sometimes student) prompt. The prompt can be in the form of a question, a problem to be solved, or a quotation. The purpose of the prompt is to engage students with the content of the course. In online course management systems like Desire2Learn or Blackboard, the instructor can track and grade student responses in the forum through a rubric. Students feel other human beings are interacting with each other, including the faculty member, which creates a sense of social presence for the students. Unfortunately, social presence alone is not enough for a class discussion. Empty responses like, "That was a great idea, Jerry," are not sufficient. Rubrics help to avoid that problem by making it clear that both quantity and quality count. Rubrics also clarify what is meant by good-quality, substantive responses. And, of course, knowing that their contributions to the forum discussions will be graded, a point emphasized by the rubric, tells students that this is an important activity, and, yes, the quality and even the tone of their responses matters. Student engagement is at the heart of a healthy and vital online discussion. Rubrics further both the quantity and quality of student responses and contribute to a healthy and respectful climate and a positive social presence for all.

Teaching Presence

Rubrics help to make it more evident that the teacher is present in the course. One way we show our presence is when we create and present an organized course with clear written assignments, activities, and assessments. The use of rubrics communicates that the professor is present and seeks to help students know how he or she is grading. Online rubrics offer the same benefits to students as they do in face-to-face classes. A well-crafted rubric is linked to course objectives and shows how completion of the assignment meets course objectives.

Rubrics show students that the professor is organized enough not only to write a narrative assignment description but also to show them how the professor will grade it. Rubrics help students focus their effort. Openness and clarity of assessment expectations build trust even when students don't see the professor face-to-face. In addition, rubrics feed into student perceptions about the fairness and organization of the grading system. Rubrics tell students that the professor is using the same standards for scoring all student work. Just as in face-to-face instruction, rubrics also help clarify the assignment, resulting in fewer questions. In the case of online instruction, this means less frustration and fewer e-mails from distressed students, a positive for students and professors alike. Without rubrics in an online environment, professors will spend a lot of time on the computer dealing with student confusion. With rubrics, it is clearer that the teacher is present, gives feedback, and responds to student work.

Cognitive Presence

Cognitive presence includes the feedback students receive on their individual assignments as well as the opportunity for students to demonstrate their thinking in and contribution to online discussions. Responding to student work online is not like making a pencil mark on their papers. If the professor uses a rubric (to define standards) and also uses Track Changes, students will get copious feedback on their written work. This means that either the professor or the students' peers are paying attention, challenging their thinking (cognitions), and pushing them to do their best work.

Conclusion

In face-to-face instruction many things are accomplished verbally and through body language. Although in face-to-face much of the content is written (e.g., syllabus, rubrics, textbooks and other materials), students come to class and engage with the professor and other students. There is a dependence on the verbal and visual cues. Loss of these typical face-to-face prompts can be disconcerting for an instructor new to online instruction. To prepare for online instruction, the professor has to elaborate in writing many of the things he or she used to just explain in class, and students need those written explanations to do the course work. Things like a full task description, how and where online groups might meet and how they communicate with one another, and how students treat each other on the discussion forum need to be explained in much more detail online than in face-to-face instruction. Rubrics are one tool that helps professors structure their assignments and engage students clearly and more fully in online learning.

Rubrics support the sense of social, teaching, and cognitive presence online, and thereby strengthen communication with students online. Rubrics are a successful and essential ingredient in online instruction.

10

RUBRICS AND TEACHING IMPROVEMENT

Teaching. Most faculty members teach to some degree. For some, it's their main activity and their careers depend on doing it well. For others, it's a relatively small addition to research, grant getting, administrative duties, and a plethora of other activities. For most, it's somewhere in between. But regardless of where teaching falls in the overall scope of their professional lives, most faculty care about teaching. They think it's important, and they want to do it well.

We have already shown some of the ways in which rubrics can improve teaching through assuring more fair, more consistent grading, and more immediate, clearly enunciated feedback. We have also shown how making rubric construction an interactive classroom activity can become a part of the educational process.

In this chapter, we look at two more ways in which rubrics can be used to reflect on teaching, and specifically how to use the information rubrics offer to improve what happens in the classroom:

- using rubric dimensions to organize notes taken while grading, and
- creating an "expanded grade book" to allow for analysis of scores using rubric dimensions.

We also include a teaching model to show how rubrics thread through all phases of teaching, demonstrating the links among student rubric scores, teaching practice, and student learning.

Horton Uses a Rubric: A Case Study

Horton, a professor in the School of Business, had attended a summer workshop where he learned to create and use a rubric for a small senior seminar, SBA 490, which he taught every year. Horton was concerned that at least some of his students in this class were not learning what he was trying to teach, a serious matter since SBA 490 was a prerequisite for SBA 491, their final senior project. He hoped that using a rubric would alleviate some of his concerns. Horton had created a rubric for the main assignment for SBA 490 (see Figure 10.1), a literature review for the students' proposed senior project. He introduced his rubric early in the semester, presenting it and encouraging students to ask questions about it. The discussion had been lively and, he hoped, informative. When his students turned in their first drafts about a third of the way through the semester, he felt confident that the results would be better than they had been the previous year without the rubric.

And at first, Horton was pleased with the new rubric. He found it allowed him to get through the drafts more rapidly, and he was sure that he was grading consistently and fairly. However, he began to realize that the overall quality of the papers had improved a little bit. The rubric was working for him, but not, apparently, as well as he hoped for his students.

Horton called Emiko at the Center for Teaching and Learning and asked for assistance.

"One idea that others have used and found helpful is to make notes on the strengths and weaknesses of the papers while you grade so that you can communicate those problems to students and note them yourself in your teaching," Emiko said.

"Hmm, how does that work?"

"Let me explain. You can use the dimensions you created for your rubric."

"Do you mean make a grid and slot the notes under whatever dimension I think they best refer to?"

"Exactly," Emiko told him. "That way your notes will be grouped automatically under each dimension so you can look for patterns."

Using Rubric Dimensions to Organize Notes Taken While Grading

Horton used a grid using the dimensions as headers for the columns, and by the time he finished, it looked like Figure 10.2.

The first thing Horton noticed when he reviewed his gridded notes was that most of his critical notes were in the final row, the Writing

Literature Review Rubric: SBA 490—Research Foundations

Task Description: You are to find at least 10 research articles related to your senior project topic. You will write a 5- to 10-page review of these articles that shows how they relate to and contribute to your understanding of your topic. This paper will lead to the development of your senior research project to be completed in SBA 491.

Dimensions	Exceeds expectations (4)	Meets expectations (3)	Needs some improvement (2)	Needs substantial improvement (1)	Not evident (0)
Problem	Introductory paragraph describes the problem clearly. Introduction engages reader with problem. Many details and descriptive words used. Thesis is clear in first few paragraphs.	Problem is clearly stated. Attempt to engage the reader, but not persuasive. Thesis is clear in first few paragraphs.	Problem was minor subject in course. Vague description of problem Weak, not persuasive thesis statement	Problem not related to any ideas in the course No clear introduction to paper, just starts with literature review	
Research articles	All peer-reviewed references At least 10 references All research articles Variety of journals used	Mostly peer-reviewed 8–10 references Mostly research articles	A few peer-reviewed 5–8 references Some books included	Mostly books and magazines used 1–5 references	
Flow	Arranges ideas from articles in a logical way. Judicious use of information from articles to make case Organization of ideas from articles evident Transition sentences used Paragraphs have topic sentences.	Mostly logical flow from idea to idea Organization evident with some gaps Some sections do not have transition sentences. Paragraphs have topic sentences.	Difficult to follow line of thinking from paragraph to paragraph Careless use of information from articles Paragraphs lack topic sentences and transitions.	Difficult to follow line of thinking Ideas from articles not in writer's own words Choppy to read aloud Paragraphs lack topic sentences and transitions.	
Conclusion	Synthesizes key ideas from literature reviewed. Relates closely to problem through thesis statement.	Synthesizes key ideas from literature reviewed. Inferred link to problem	Synthesizes a few ideas. Slight link to problem	No synthesis Problem not mentioned	
Writing conventions	Perfect APA formatting in text and in reference list 1 grammatical error	2–3 minor errors in APA formatting 2–3 grammatical errors	Noticeable lack of attention to APA Grammatical errors interfere with reading	No APA formatting Many grammatical errors on every page make reading difficult.	

Figure 10.1 Horton's literature review rubric.

Assignment Dimensions	What students did on various aspects of the assignment	What I can do next time: Changes in instruction and this assignment
Problem	Problem Engaging introduction ✓✓✓✓ Clear, rich description ✓✓✓✓✓ Thesis clear ✓✓✓✓✓✓✓✓	Those examples I shared in class seemed to help with the introduction. It was great to read and shows they are engaged in their topic.
Research articles	Mostly peer-reviewed ✓✓ Few peer-reviewed ✓✓✓✓✓✓✓✓✓✓✓	Still trouble identifying peer-reviewed articles Bring in librarian to show how to find these.

Flow	Logical flow through articles
	Choppy
	Transitions:
	   Used well
	   Missing
	Topic sentences:
	   Used well
	   Need work
	Writing . . .
		Some seem to have the idea here. Others need work on the flow from paragraph to paragraph.
		Get Writing Center folks in here earlier next term. I hope my feedback helps for the next draft.

Conclusion	Synthesizes key ideas from research article review Clearly relates these to problem and thesis statement	Most can synthesize, but linking back directly to the problem and thesis still a problem. Provide examples?

Writing conventions	APA formatting:
	   In text
	   In reference list
	Grammar
	Page numbers
		Still need some work here on APA. Find a YouTube video to put on course management system, plus share links to the OWL Purdue website that seems to do a good job of this.

Figure 10.2   Horton's notes jotted down while grading literature review papers.

Conventions dimension, and also that most of them referred to issues with APA formatting. He also realized that, just by writing out the strengths and weaknesses of the papers, he was already thinking of some solutions, of some way to improve his teaching, given his notes on the specific rubric dimensions.

Learning to use APA formatting was important for his students, he thought, not just because of the way it would affect their grades in this and other classes, but also because most of them planned to enter the world of business one way or another. There, it would be important for them to be able to master and use a variety of writing and citation formats.

He called Emiko to tell her that her strategy had been successful in helping him identify some areas where the students needed specific help and where he could adjust his teaching to meet their needs.

She was pleased that the strategy had worked, but she wondered whether formatting errors alone could be the whole cause of students underperforming, as Horton had expressed in their earlier conversation.

"There are other things you can do with your rubric to understand more about what's going on with your class," she told him. "Why don't you come see me tomorrow and I'll show you some. Bring your notes, your grade book, and the scored student rubrics, the ones where you've already circled or checked the descriptions of dimensions to let your students know how well they've succeeded in meeting expectations."

Creating an "Expanded Grade Book"

Horton had already returned the papers by the time he met with Emiko, but he had carefully made copies of the finished rubrics. He was surprised when she suggested they look first at his grade book. He thought she would want to see the rubrics.

"We'll get back to the rubrics," she assured him, "but first let's see what we can do with the grade book alone. I see you've only entered the final scores derived from the rubric."

"What else would I put in my grade book except grades?"

"But you haven't put all the scores on each dimension from the rubric that make up the final grade for each student," Emiko pointed out, "just the final grade. Your grade book can tell you much more about what's going on with your class if we expand it using your rubric."

Emiko re-created Horton's grade book on a grid, inserting the rubric dimensions at the top, with the last column being the final total points, then she added columns next to the names for each of the dimensions. It was still a grade book, but an expanded version of what he had been using before. The names of the students she left as they were, down the side, opposite their final grades, as shown in Figure 10.1, but, as shown in Figure 10.3, the expanded grade book included how each student did on each dimension.

Emiko explained that even when each dimension is accorded separate points on a rubric, most faculty members log only the aggregated

Student number	Problem	Research articles	Flow	Conclusion	Writing conventions	TOTAL
1. Sam	4	4	4	4	4	20
2. Hercules	4	3	3	2	4	16
3. Josie	4	3	3	4	4	18
4. Juanita	3	2	1	1	1	8
5. Henry	4	4	3	4	1	16
6. Harriet	4	1	4	3	4	16
7. Ernie	4	3	3	1	3	14
8. Juan	3	2	2	1	2	10
9. Anita	2	2	3	1	2	10
10. Jessie	2	3	1	2	2	10

4 = Exceeds expectations; 3 = Meets expectations; 2 = Needs improvement; 1 = Needs substantial improvement; 0 = Not evident

Figure 10.3 Horton's expanded grade book with rubric scores disaggregated by dimensions.

number, that is, a number that is composed of the different scores on each dimension of the rubric. Faculty members are quite accustomed to looking across the grade book to follow a student's work over the term, but they seldom keep records of the component points from rubric dimensions that went into that final score.

Emiko and Horton used the copies of the finished rubrics to enter the exact points each student had received in any given dimension.

The first thing Horton noticed was that this method gave him more insight into individual student learning. Three students—Hercules (Student #2), Henry (#5) and Harriet (#6)—had all received an aggregate score of 16, but that was the only similarity in their work. Hercules lost most of his points in the conclusion dimension, whereas Henry lost his points in the writing conventions, and Harriet lost most of her points on her selection of research articles.

"Wow! That final score sure masks where the problems are," Horton commented. "They had the same final score but arrived there differently."

"And you can use that knowledge to help them differently when you talk to them one-on-one," Emiko agreed. "Now try looking at the columns separately."

"There are a lot of low scores in the Conclusion column," said Horton. "I didn't notice that when I was taking notes. I mean, I noticed some problems, but not that they were so much more pronounced in that dimension than in the others. Hmm. I have an idea about how to work on that. I have some examples of good conclusions in my files; I should pass those out and maybe do some in-class exercises."

Emiko nodded. "The Flow column doesn't look too healthy either."

"I think I'll have the Writing Center folks in to work with my class," Horton sighed.

"And some of your students still don't seem to understand what peer-reviewed articles are," Emiko added.

"Or don't know how to find them," Horton agreed. "I've explained it several times. I'm not sure what's not getting through."

"Sometimes hands-on works best. Have you taken them through the process of searching the databases and identifying peer-reviewed articles?"

Horton shook his head. "I could schedule a class in the computer labs though," he added.

"Be sure to show the Writing Center people your expanded grade book," Emiko advised, "so they know where to focus. That's another asset to having disaggregated the scores from each dimension on the rubric. It's easier to communicate your exact concerns to others."

"And the better we all understand what's going on, the better we can do our jobs. I like looking for these patterns in the rubric dimension scores," Horton concluded.

A Teaching Model: Four Phases of Teaching

Before Horton left her office, Emiko handed him a basic teaching model (Figure 10.4) to show how he used the results of his disaggregated data. Emiko noted, "This is called a concept map and it lays out four essential teaching phases: reflect, plan, teach, and assess."

"It looks a lot like the four stages we went through to create the rubric," said Horton.

"I can see why you say that," Emiko told him. "However, this is different. The rubric development stages are reflect, list, group/label, and apply. Developing a rubric is a step-by-step sequential plan in

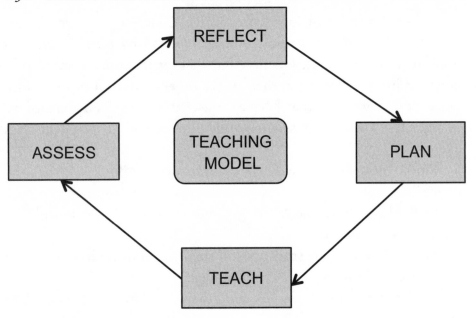

Figure 10.4 A teaching model.

which each new stage builds on the previous one, and you end up with a final product, a rubric. One key component in rubric development and the teaching model, however, is reflection."

"Even though there is a logical order to the teaching model," she told Horton, "and the phases appear as separate steps, in reality these phases are interdependent and often blend into one another. For example, while you teach, you also reflect about how well things are going. Just like today, while we've been disaggregating rubric scores and reflecting on teaching practices, we've also done a lot of planning. This model may help you expand on what we have done and think of other ways to use the rubric and rubric scores."

She explained, "The teaching model is certainly not the only way to conceptualize teaching. Yet, it illustrates the different activities that a professor goes through in creating, delivering, and assessing a course. Since it is a map of the "teaching territory," so to speak, it does not display all the details of teaching, but it distills the essential features and identifies separate activities that a professor goes through before, during, and after teaching."

A month later, Horton reappeared in Emiko's office to report that the second drafts had been greatly improved, and to give her a present,

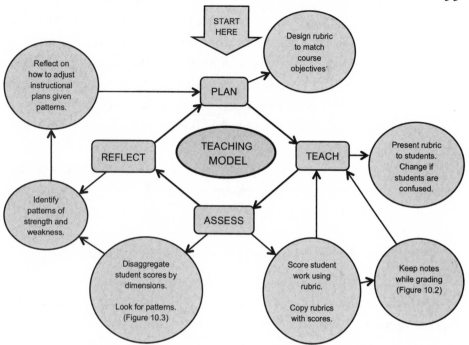

Figure 10.5   A teaching model with ways to use rubrics to improve instruction.

a greatly expanded version of the teaching model she had given him, portrayed in Figure 10.5.

Horton explained that his expanded model illustrated how he had integrated his new understandings of his teaching by using his rubric results and his expanded grade book. He had added circular bubbles outside the inner boxes of the Teaching Model that showed the role his rubrics had played at each phase.

The Teaching Model: Reflect

Horton had been intrigued by what his disaggregated rubric scores showed him about his individual students and about the class as a whole. He noted that his usual pattern of reflection on his classes involved looking at individual students to see how each of them was doing. Disaggregating their total scores in his expanded grade book offered him clearer insights into each student's strengths and weaknesses.

The expanded grade book also allowed him to look at the class as a whole, identifying the places where the strengths and weaknesses revealed as much about his teaching as it did about each student's personal learning. That had been apparent even at the start when he used his dimensions to take notes as he graded, but it was even clearer when he laid out the specific scores each student received on each dimension on a grid in his expanded grade book. Then he had only to look down each column to see how well or poorly the majority of the class was doing in each dimension.

He had expanded on that quick visual assessment of the scores by making a list of questions he asked himself as he went down each column, looking for patterns:

✓ How did students do overall on the different assignments?

✓ On which dimension did most of my students score well? Which dimensions have the lowest scores? What does that tell me about my teaching? What do I need to change to improve their work?

✓ How well did the rubric work? Any confusing parts? Do I need to add anything or rewrite phrases?

Those three basic questions led Horton to a self-assessment of the rubric scores in light of how the class was taught and how the students responded to instruction. He reflected on what those patterns meant, and what specific skills were involved in each dimension of his rubric, and then he decided what strategy to employ and whether to use other resources on campus. If his students were not able to cite sources accurately, he wondered, was that something he should devote more time to, or would it be better to ask the Writing Center or the librarians to have a go at it? If he decided to use an outside resource like the library, he would have to adjust the schedule and quite probably fail to cover some other material he had hoped to cover. Were the weaknesses serious enough for him to do that? The disaggregated rubric scores offered a richer and more complex view of student learning that allowed him to make that decision.

The Teaching Model: Plan

His analysis of the rubric data affected his teaching plans. In fact, Horton decided to make some immediate changes in his schedule and even some smaller assignments. Writing issues, he decided, were basic and so was the fact that so many students were not accurately identifying peer-reviewed material. Faced with evidence that his class was having trouble with not one but two aspects of writing ("flow" and "conclusions"), Horton canceled one whole class to allow the Writing Center to go over some of these issues. He also set aside half of another class period for in-class peer reviewing of conclusions. And he canceled yet a third planned lecture to allow for a session in the computer labs, where he intended to take his students step-by-step through the databases to make sure they knew how to use them and how to identify what was and what was not a peer-reviewed source.

And, to ensure that his students would take the new additions to the course seriously, Horton cancelled two smaller assignments having to do with creating graphs and charts (he actually punted them up the line to SBA 491, which he also taught), and announced that he would be grading the peer reviewing of the conclusions, and the list of at least five peer-reviewed articles that students would find during the computer lab session on databases.

The Teaching Model: Teach

In light of his new plans, Horton adjusted what he taught and when he relied on the expertise of others. Horton did not, in fact, "teach" two of the three new classes he incorporated into his schedule. The Writing Center taught one of them, and when Horton called to book the library computer lab so he could take his class through the intricacies of a database search, he discovered that one of the librarians routinely offered such a class.

That offered Horton a unique opportunity to reflect on what "teaching" and "learning" was going on, because he was only marginally involved. He was able to be more alert than usual to the questions his students asked, to the expressions on their faces that revealed whether the answers they received were actually helpful, and what confusion kept resurfacing. Later, he found himself more aware of such matters while he himself was teaching classes, meeting with students, grading student papers, giving feedback, holding office hours, and interacting with students both inside and outside class.

As he listened, he also realized how both the Writing Center instructor and the librarian referred to the rubric from time to time, thus linking their information to the students' potential grades. Horton noticed there was still some confusion there, too, which he noted and addressed later in class. The following year, he also used those notes to improve the rubric itself.

The Teaching Model: Assess

Horton believed that the changes he made in the classroom should be reflected in new assessment data from the student rubric scores. He was excited to see how all of this attention to reflecting, planning, and teaching using his rubric scores would work out. Most of Horton's assessment took place a month later, when his students turned in their second drafts.

Overall, Horton was pleased. The second drafts had dramatically improved over the first, and boded well for the final version. Before his session with Emiko and his use of the teaching model, he might well have left matters there, based on his global assessment of each student's work and the feedback he provided them individually through his rubric and other notes.

Now, however, he added a second level in which he examined the whole set of student data to assess how well the course was going and what further instructional changes he might need to make. In the course of that deeper assessment, using his rubric dimensions, disaggregated data, and expanded grade book, he also made an unexpected discovery: the four students whose work continued to show real problems all came from families in which they were the first to attend college. He made a note of that and added it to his planning for the following year. In the short run, he also scheduled a meeting with a colleague in the sociology department whose research focused on such students.

Conclusion

So what can rubrics tell us about teaching? Certainly rubrics help students. However, analyzing the rubric and student scores on the rubric dimensions enables you to identify the areas of strength and weakness in student work, both individually and collectively. Analysis of disaggregated rubric scores leads to questions such as:

✓ In what dimensions are students as a group successful?

✓ In what dimensions are students as a group not so successful?

✓ What instructional changes might I make to improve student performance in a particular dimension?

✓ What parts of the rubric do I need to rewrite to add clarity, and what parts seem to work well?

✓ Are there subgroups or individual students who may need special help?

The goal here is to find the patterns of performance across the class and not focus so much on the individual student. Disaggregating the dimensions and going across the grade book and looking at individual scores, and looking down the grade book columns helps faculty members to begin to see the patterns of variance in their classes. Those patterns lead to questions and concerns as well as pats on the back.

The thoughtful use of rubrics and rubric data can improve teaching, and students can benefit from that improvement. Rubrics offer a wealth of information depending on how they are used and how the data from the rubric are laid out. This is one very good example of data-driven decision making. After all, rubric scores are professors' own data from their own students, with their own rubrics, and in their own classes. As we have shown in this chapter, these data can propel powerful insights and reflections that make teaching more satisfying for the professor and more worthwhile for students.

Horton is not alone in discovering the value of reflecting on rubric scores as data to improve teaching. As we show in Chapter 11, faculty members have used rubrics as a data source for scholarly teaching projects that can result in publications that benefit others as well benefiting writers themselves.

II

RUBRICS FOR SELF-ASSESSMENT AND CAREER ADVANCEMENT

A new job. Annual reports. Tenure. Promotion. These are stress points in any faculty member's professional life, events that can make or break a promising career. And they all require documentation that the faculty member is expected to create—not just letters of recommendation, teaching evaluations, or a list of publications, but often a "teaching philosophy statement," a "reflection on teaching and scholarship," or some other narrative regarding the faculty member's claim to be a scholar and teacher. That narrative is a major component in whether an application for a new job, tenure, or promotion is successful. Yet most universities are vague when it comes to what that narrative is expected to contain and give few if any guidelines. Everyone is expected to know. Colleagues and mentors can help, but the situation is not unlike that facing students who come into academe from non-academic backgrounds: there are tacit expectations that require explanation, sometimes "translation," of academic language. As with those students, rubrics can help to clear away some of the fog. In this chapter, we look at three rubrics that have been used successfully to write about professional life in three different contexts:

- Developing a teaching philosophy statement
- Reflecting on teaching with an eye toward sharing that reflection with others
- Writing the narrative for a promotion and tenure portfolio

Writing such narratives is essential for career advancement, but it has other benefits as well. Writing about aspects of professional life also affirms the links among theories, beliefs, and practices and, this, in turn, builds a vocabulary and a way to describe faculty work that more readily persuades others of one's expertise. There is also a personal benefit. Producing a narrative of a professor's own evolution as a scholar and teacher, of his or her own values that are embedded in professional practice, often leads to rich insights that are personally satisfying, enlightening, and empowering. Done well, such writing and reflection becomes "a distinctive organizing vision—a clear picture of why you are doing what you are doing that you can call up at points of crisis . . ." (Brookfield, 1990, p. 16).

Rubric for Writing a Teaching Philosophy Statement

Almost all dossiers for new academic jobs, annual reports, and tenure and promotion decisions require a "statement of teaching philosophy," but few spell out precisely what that is. One notable exception is the "rubric for composing and evaluating a statement of teaching philosophy" developed by the University of Michigan, Ann Arbor, Center for Research on Learning and Teaching (CRLT) for university teaching assistants (see Figure 11.1).

Deborah Meizlish and Matt Kaplan (2008), directors of the University of Michigan CRLT, devised their rubric from research and practice. In their research, they examined job descriptions and surveyed chairs of search committees to better understand the role a teaching philosophy statement played in their decision-making. From their research, Meizlish and Kaplan determined that job candidates are well served by devoting careful attention to these statements. From 908 job descriptions across several disciplines in a variety of higher education institutions, they found that some form of a philosophy of teaching statement was a required part of about 33% of the applications for a faculty position. Whether required or not, about 60% of search committee chairs reported using teaching statements during at least some portion of the hiring process. Even when not required, Meizlish and Kaplan found that 100% of these faculty search committee chairs generally appreciated the inclusion of a teaching philosophy statement. The burgeoning research literature affirms the fact that across all levels of higher education institutions, a teaching philosophy statement is becoming more and more critical to hiring (Kaplan, Meizlish, O'Neal, & Wright, 2008; Schönwetter, Taylor, & Ellis, 2006).

Categories	Excellent	Needs some revision	Unsatisfactory
Goals for student learning: What knowledge, skills, and attitudes are important for student success in your discipline? What are you preparing students for? What are the key challenges in the teaching-learning process?	Goals are clearly articulated, specific, and go beyond knowledge level, including skills, attitudes, career goals, etc. Goals are sensitive to the context of the instructor's discipline. They are concise, not exhaustive.	Goals are articulated but may be too broad or not specific to the discipline. Goals focus on basic knowledge, ignoring skills acquisition and affective change.	Articulation of goals is unfocused, incomplete, or missing.
Enactment of goals (teaching methods): What teaching methods do you use? How do these methods contribute to your goals for students? Why are these methods appropriate for use in your discipline?	Enactment of goals is specific and thoughtful, includes details and rationale for teaching methods. The methods are clearly connected to specific goals and are appropriate for those goals. Specific examples of the methods in use within the disciplinary context are given.	Description of teaching methods not clearly connected to goals or, if connected, not well developed (seems like a list of what is done in the classroom). Methods are described but generically; no example of the instructor's use of the methods within the discipline is communicated.	Enactment of goals is not articulated. If there is an attempt to articulate teaching methods, it is basic and unreflective.
Assessment of goals (measuring student learning): How do you know your goals for students are being met? What sorts of assessment tools do you use (tests, papers, portfolios, journals) and why? How do assessments contribute to student learning? How do assessments communicate disciplinary priorities?	Specific examples of assessment tools are clearly described. Assessment tools are aligned with teaching goals and teaching methods. Assessments reinforce the priorities and context of the discipline in both content and type.	Assessments are described, but not connected to goals and teaching methods. Description is too general, with no reference to the motivation behind the assessments. There is no clear connection between the assessments and the priorities of the discipline.	Assessments of goals are not articulated or are mentioned only in passing.
Creating an inclusive learning environment, addressing one or more of the following questions: How do your own and your students' identities (e.g., race, gender, class), backgrounds, experiences, and levels of privilege affect the classroom? How do you take into account the diverse learning styles? How do you integrate diverse perspectives into your teaching?	Portrays a coherent philosophy of inclusive education that is integrated throughout the statement. Makes space for diverse ways of knowing and/or learning styles. Discussion of roles is sensitive to historically underrepresented students. Demonstrates awareness of issues of equity within the discipline.	Inclusive teaching is addressed but in a cursory manner or in a way that isolates it from the rest of the philosophy. Author briefly connects identity issues to aspects of his or her teaching.	Issues of inclusion are not addressed or are addressed in an awkward manner. There is no connection to teaching.
Structure, rhetoric, and language: How is the reader engaged? Is the language used appropriate to the discipline? How is the statement thematically structured?	The statement has a guiding structure and/or theme that engages the reader and organizes the goals, methods, and assessments articulated in the statement. Jargon is avoided and teaching terms (e.g., critical thinking) are given specific definitions that apply to the instructor's disciplinary context. Grammar and spelling are correct.	The statement has a structure and/or theme that is not connected to the ideas actually discussed in the statement, or organizing structure is weak and does not resonate within the disciplinary context. The statement contains some jargon.	No overall structure present. Statement is a collection of disconnected statements about teaching. Jargon is used liberally and not supported by specific definitions or examples. Needs much revision.

Figure 11.1 Rubric for composing and evaluating statements of teaching philosophy from Center for Research on Learning and Teaching, University of Michigan. Reprinted with permission, www.crlt.umich.edu/sites/default/files/resource_filesTeachingPhilosophyRubric.pdf.

In practice, along with many other academic institutions, the Center for Research on Learning and Teaching (CRLT) at the University of Michigan in Ann Arbor provides assistance and feedback to doctoral students as they develop their teaching philosophy statements. The rubric for writing the teaching philosophy statement was developed over the years using the literature on best teaching practices and the center's experience working with and reading hundreds of teaching philosophy statements. Occasional Paper No. 23, available from the CRLT center, guides graduate students' initial thinking about writing such a document (www.crlt.umich.edu/publinks/pub links.php).

The CRLT teaching philosophy rubric (Figure 11.1) has five dimensions (or categories). Under each dimension is a set of questions that helps teaching assistants focus on developing that dimension of their philosophy. The resulting statement is only 1–2 pages long. CRLT uses this rubric in numerous ways. In their Preparing Future Faculty Programs, graduate students first become familiar with the rubric by using it to score and discuss other sample teaching philosophies. They then use it to provide peer feedback on each other's draft statements. In the Center's Graduate Teacher Certificate program, specially trained graduate student consultants use the rubric to provide feedback and then "certify" a graduate student's completion of the teaching statement portion of the certificate requirement.

The teaching philosophy rubric is not just for scoring the statement but is meant to further reflection and writing. Certainly the final philosophy statement can be used in a job search, but the rubric also guides the graduate teaching assistant toward reflecting on what best practice in teaching includes.

It also has much to offer more advanced faculty members as they prepare annual reviews as well as applications for tenure and promotion. The University of Michigan CRLT's teaching philosophy statement rubric indicates a number of different dimensions that can be used to think about teaching and to express the various ways teaching affects student learning. The dimensions describe familiar aspects of teaching: goals for student learning, teaching methods, assessment practices, and evidence of an inclusive classroom in which learning actually takes place.

Rubric for the Scholar-Educator

The University of Michigan rubric for writing a teaching philosophy statement is easily adapted to serve the needs of newly hired faculty. Similarly, even though the "Expertise Levels of a Scientist-Educator" rubric (Bernstein et al., 2009) was initially designed for experienced faculty members who seek to self-assess and improve their teaching, it is also suitable for newly hired faculty members. Although it references "scientist-educators," it might just as easily be called a "scholar-educator" rubric because it focuses on teaching and scholarship in a universal fashion.

A comparison of the University of Michigan teaching philosophy (Figure 11.1) and the scholar-educator rubric (Figure 11.2) shows how versatile rubrics are. These two rubrics cover similar content area but have different purposes, as indicated by the different dimensions, levels of performance, and the target audience that uses the rubric. In Figure 11.1 the dimensions are called "categories," whereas in Figure 11.2 they are called "components." Even though the words are different, each demonstrates that complex tasks can be better understood when they are divided into different subtasks, the dimensions. Both assist professors or future professors in analyzing their teaching. A comparison of the similarities and differences provides insight into how rubrics can be about the same topic, yet can emphasize different aspects of the whole task and can be used for different reasons. The first one results in a teaching philosophy statement. The second one, the scholar-educator rubric, furthers an analysis of teaching practice that can have several outcomes, from a deep personal reflection on teaching to a foundation for a publication about teaching.

As we continue our comparison of both rubrics, the scholar-educator rubric covers many of the same teaching elements as the University of Michigan rubric. It includes the usual aspects of teaching: goals for student learning, teaching methods, assessment practices, and evidence of an inclusive classroom. However, this scholar-educator (S-E) rubric adds three separate dimensions not found at this level of detail in the teaching philosophy rubric. These are "Preparation for the course or learning activity," "Reflection on the teaching and its impact on student learning," and "Communication of teaching results to others."

Components	Entry into teaching	Basic skill	Professional	Advanced
Goals of the course or other learning activity	Course/activity goals are absent, unclear, or inappropriate.	Course/activity goals are well articulated and appropriate to the courses and the curriculum.	Course/activity goals identify intellectually challenging and/or enduring targets and/or are especially well matched to students.	Course/activity goals identify levels of performance that represent excellence and are of interest to many stakeholders.
Preparation for the course or learning activity	Teacher is not adequately knowledgeable and/or has no background in teaching.	The teaching is based on prior scholarship in its area, including current content as well as pedagogical methods and conceptual frames.	The teacher's preparation includes broad synthesis of prior work in content as well as practice in pedagogical methods and conceptual frames.	The teacher acquires and integrates knowledge and skills drawn from the literature of multiple disciplines, in both content and pedagogy.
Methods used to conduct the teaching	No apparent rationale for teaching methods used; there is no instructional design.	The work follows the conventions of teaching practices within its domain of discipline and institution.	The teaching takes full advantage of effective methods discussed within its discipline.	The work generates new practices that will enable others to improve or enhance their teaching.
Evidence gathered to demonstrate the impact of the teacher's work	There is no measure of student learning, or assessment methods do not match espoused goals.	There is evidence linking students' performances to espoused goals.	Student performances indicate that deep and/or broad learning is taking place.	The learning demonstrated is exemplary in depth of learning and/or in breadth of students' success.
Reflection on the teaching and its impact on student learning	The teacher provides no indication of having reflected upon or learned from prior teaching.	The teacher articulates lessons learned from reflecting on prior teaching.	The teacher has examined the impact on students' performance within a conceptual framework and adjusted practice based on reflection.	Enhanced achievement of learning goals results from reflection on evidence within a conceptual framework, or teacher revises conceptual framework based on student learning outcomes.
Communication of teaching results to others	The practices and results of teaching are kept private.	The teacher's work and students' performances are publicly accessible for others to use, to build upon, and to review critically.	The teacher's reflective work has been read and cited by others who have provided commentary and feedback.	The teacher's work has had a broad impact on the practices and inquiry of many others interested in the same teaching practices and questions.

Figure 11.2 Scholar-educator (renamed for this work from "scientist-educator") rubric, derived from Bernstein et al. (2009). Copyright ©2009 by the American Psychological Association. Reproduced with permission.

In relation to the teaching philosophy rubric, the two dimensions in the S-E rubric, "Preparation for the course or learning activity" and "Reflection on the teaching and its impact on student learning," greatly expand on the specific actions and reflections that faculty members can examine and act on to improve student learning. Some of these actions are described in the S-E rubric as using the knowledge from others in the discipline to improve teaching practices, analyzing evidence of learning from student work, and reflecting on student learning data in relation to overall student learning outcomes.

Another difference between the two rubrics is that the labels for performance levels reveal contrasting purposes. For the teaching philosophy rubric, on one hand, the levels are "Excellent," "Needs some revision," and "Unsatisfactory." Clearly these are designed to push the writer to the excellent level, which is really the only acceptable level. Teaching philosophy statements specify a mastery level that all should attain. The highest level is in the first column after the dimensions to draw the eye to that expectation.

The levels on the scholar-educator rubric, on the other hand, "Entry into teaching," "Basic skill," "Professional," and "Advanced," indicate that teaching is a developmental process. Most do not start out "advanced," and professors should not necessarily expect to be there. However, over time, professors can strive toward that higher and more complex teaching practice. The levels of performance in the scholar-educator rubric show the faculty member that learning to teach takes time. It is significant that the levels are presented in developmental order, with the less-complex or more-traditional teaching level first and the more-complex and less-traditional teaching levels following as the eye moves from level to level, left to right.

The greatest difference between the two rubrics, however, is the inclusion of the final dimension in the scholar-educator rubric: "Communication of teaching results to others." This dimension is not found in the teaching philosophy rubric. In this rubric, it applies to faculty members moving from keeping their teaching reflections to themselves to submitting their research and insights to others for peer review. These may mean a refereed publication, but the description of an advanced level of performance in this dimension could also easily include papers presented, poster presentations, reviews of work (published or not), and evidence of impact of published works from citation indexes such as Social Science Citation Index, Science Citation Index, and the more inclusive Google Scholar index.

The importance of stressing that progression was revealed in the case of a young faculty member in the mechanical engineering department; Ming, the faculty member, used the scholar-educator rubric in preparing the teaching section of his narrative statement for his first annual review. He quickly realized that his achievements in the "Methods used to conduct the teaching" dimension fell solidly into the description provided under "Basic skill: The work follows the conventions of teaching practices within its domain of discipline and institution." He described his teaching in the following narrative:

> I was taught the essential knowledge of mechanical engineering through the lecture method. It worked well for me. So, basically I lecture. There is a lot of material for students to learn. Students are pleased and often tell me that they like lecture. I put the outline of my lecture notes online so that students can follow along. This keeps them alert and they know where the lecture is going.

Even though his students seemed to like his lectures, few asked probing questions. He feared that they had, yes, learned the content but were definitely not engaged at a deeper level. He took what he had written to George, the director at the Center for Teaching and Learning, and asked for help. George began, "Thanks for coming to the center. I assure you that after only one year of teaching, no one expects you to be at an advanced level. Thinking about it, yes, but implementing new practices? Well, that can be hard when you are figuring out how to write a syllabus, make tests, and grade papers fairly and consistently as well as just how to work the copy machine. There is so much to learn about university teaching."

Ming felt relieved, but was curious. "If I wanted to do a better job at lecture, what should I do?"

George quickly replied, "I know that one of your colleagues, Akseli, regularly uses the *Journal of Engineering Education* to spark some new ideas in his teaching practice. Akseli is a full professor in the engineering department. He has let me use his teaching narrative as a sample of what reflection at the advanced level might look like.

The advanced level on the rubric states, 'The work generates new practices that will enable others to improve or enhance their teaching.'" Akseli wrote this narrative:

> Although I have been using lecture for many years in my mechanical engineering classes, after reading about new practices in engineering education journals and looking carefully at my student evaluations, I have changed some of my methods. I have added a student response system called "clickers." Students answer multiple-choice questions posted on the Power-Point by using a response board on a "clicker" that has buttons and is about the size of a cell phone. Then the system tabulates the correctness of their answers and shows these for the whole class to see. This interactive device helps students attend to my short lectures and also indicates to me what they have learned. From their answers, I can quickly tell what they do not know or have not learned. In addition, in each class I have a case study where students have to immediately apply what I just lectured about to a real-life situation. To see if this makes a difference in student learning, I have been collecting data on how well the case studies help them learn the content. My department chair has asked me to share at our next faculty meeting, to show how I use clickers and even evaluate them. He also thinks I should tell them about how I use case studies.

Reassured by his new understanding of the scholar-educator rubric's progressive approach and somewhat excited by the idea of using "clickers," Ming rewrote his narrative to include his reflections concerning the lack of deep engagement for his students and, in the following year, began to change the way he taught.

In conclusion, there are several different ways that the scholar-educator rubric can be used:

For self-reflection and action: To reflect on current practice and ask questions like: What do I do now in my teaching? At what level would I place myself on each dimension? What would I like to do in the future? Do I have the time and energy to try out some new teaching methods? Where are my students doing well? Where do they seem to be flagging? What can I do about it?

In conversation with colleagues (such as the directors and staff in centers for teaching and learning): To identify strengths as well as growth areas and ask such questions as: What books might I read to think more deeply about my teaching? What would I like to change to make my classes more engaging? What suggestions do others have for the workshops and conferences that I might attend?

As a systematic way to gather data and share with others: To take a step-by-step approach to gathering data on student learning and sharing results with others informally centered on these questions: What kind of data will tell me what students are learning? What new practices have I tried? How did students respond? What are good venues for getting ideas from others and for sharing my ideas? Department meetings? Conference roundtables?

Another unexpected use for the scholar-educator rubric is in a more formal venue, such as a publication. This rubric can be quite useful even if the professor does not want to share results publicly. However, publishing may not be the only evidence of communication within disciplines, but it remains the most universally valued. The dimensions of the scholar-educator rubric are ideal as a foundation for designing and implementing a scholarship of teaching and learning (SOTL) research project that entails the following steps:

- Set teaching goals.
- Prepare/plan the project.
- Define research methodology.
- Gather evidence.
- Reflect on it and write about what was learned.
- Communicate it through academic presentations and publication.

The time has never been better for getting such scholarly teaching projects published in discipline-specific teaching journals that are peer-reviewed and considered valid evidence when tenure and promotion are considered. Today, every academic discipline has at least one such journal that publishes research that faculty have done on their teaching, for example, *Journal of Engineering Education*, *Psychology Education*, and *Journal of Management Education*. There are even journals like the *International Journal of Scholarship of Teaching and Learning* that publish only articles related to faculty studying their teaching.

A full list of such journals across disciplines can be found at www.uww.edu/learn/journalsotl.php or
http://ilstu.libguides.com/content.php?pid=95734&sid=716042

Rubric for a Narrative for Promotion and Tenure

"Read the promotion and tenure guidelines." That's the advice most faculty members get as they prepare to make their cases to promotion and tenure (P&T) committees. It's good advice, but in practice, those guidelines are often overly wordy, cryptic, and difficult to use to structure a coherent essay. Figure 11.3 is a page from Portland State University's P&T guidelines.

In fact, Portland State's guidelines are comparatively clear, albeit wordy, but when Dannelle Stevens, coauthor of this book, went up for tenure in 1997 at PSU, she found she still had work to do to isolate those aspects that were most useful for crafting her own narrative from the 34-page Portland State Promotion and Tenure Guidelines.

She began by considering the historical context of these guidelines. In 1994 PSU laid out explicit guidelines for scholarship and for promotion and tenure following the seminal work of Ernest Boyer (1990). Boyer expanded the definition of academic scholarship to include the scholarship of discovery, integration, interpretation, and application. Too often *academic scholarship* is defined purely as "discovery." The addition of these other three areas opened up the classical notion of what counts as worthy academic work from traditional research to impact and application. To PSU, the term *scholar* "implies superior intellectual, aesthetic or creative attainment" (PSU Promotion and Tenure Guidelines, 1994, p. 5; www.pdx.edu/oaa/promotion-and-tenure-information). The expressions of such scholarship were described as:

- Research
- Teaching
- Community outreach

D. Quality and Significance of Scholarship

Quality and significance of scholarship are the primary criteria for determining faculty promotion and tenure. Quality and significance of scholarship are over-arching, integrative concepts that apply equally to the expressions of scholarship as they may appear in various disciplines and to faculty accomplishments resulting from research, teaching, and community outreach (see E.2–4).

A consistently high quality of scholarship, and its promise for future exemplary scholarship, is more important than the quantity of the work done. The criteria for evaluating the quality and significance of scholarly accomplishments include the following:

1. *Clarity and Relevance of Goals.* A scholar should clearly define objectives of scholarly work and clearly state basic questions of inquiry. Clarity of purpose provides a critical context for evaluating scholarly work.
   - Research or community outreach projects should address substantive intellectual, aesthetic, or creative problems, or issues within one's chosen discipline or interdisciplinary field. Clear objectives are necessary for fair evaluation.
   - Teaching activities are usually related to learning objectives that are appropriate within the context of curricular goals and the state of knowledge in the subject matter.

2. *Mastery of Existing Knowledge.* A scholar must be well-prepared and knowledgeable about developments in his or her field. The ability to educate others, conduct meaningful research, and provide high-quality assistance through community outreach depends upon mastering existing knowledge.
   - As researchers and problem solvers, scholars propose methodologies, measures, and interventions that reflect relevant theory, conceptualizations, and cumulative wisdom.
   - As teachers, scholars demonstrate a command of resources and exhibit a depth, breadth, and understanding of subject matter allowing them to respond adequately to student learning needs and to evaluate teaching and curricular innovation.

3. *Appropriate Use of Methodology and Resources.* A scholar should address goals with carefully constructed logic and methodology.
   - Rigorous research and applied problem solving requires well-constructed methodology that allows one to determine the efficacy of the tested hypotheses or chosen intervention.
   - As teachers, scholars apply appropriate pedagogy and instructional techniques to maximize student learning and use appropriate methodology to evaluate the effectiveness of curricular activities.

4. *Effectiveness of Communication.* Scholars should possess effective oral and written communication skills that enable them to convert knowledge into language that a public audience beyond the classroom, research laboratory, or field site can understand.
   - As researchers and problem solvers, scholars make formal oral presentations and write effective manuscripts or reports or create original artistic works that

Figure 11.3   Portland State University Promotion and Tenure Guidelines, 1994, 2006, pp. 6–7. Reprinted with permission, 1996, 2006, Portland State University, Promotion and Tenure Guidelines.

meet the professional standards of the intended audience. As teachers, scholars communicate in ways that build positive student rapport and clarify new knowledge so as to facilitate learning. They also should be able to disseminate the results of their curricular innovations to their teaching peers.

- Scholars should communicate with appropriate audiences and subject their ideas to critical inquiry and independent review. Usually the results of scholarship are communicated widely through publications (e.g., journal articles and books), performances, exhibits, and/or presentations at conferences and workshops.

5. *Significance of Results.* Scholars should evaluate whether or not they achieve their goals and whether or not this achievement had an important impact on and is used by others. Customarily, peers and other multiple and credible sources (e.g., students, community participants, and subject matter experts) evaluate the significance of results.

- As researchers, teachers, and problem solvers, scholars widely disseminate their work in order to invite scrutiny and to measure varying degrees of critical acclaim. They must consider more than direct user satisfaction when evaluating the quality and significance of an intellectual contribution.
- Faculty engaged in community outreach can make a difference in their communities and beyond by defining or resolving relevant social problems or issues, by facilitating organizational development, by improving existing practices or programs, and by enriching the cultural life of the community. Scholars should widely disseminate the knowledge gained in a community-based project in order to share its significance with those who do not benefit directly from the project.
- As teachers, scholars can make a difference in their students' lives by raising student motivation to learn, by developing students' life-long learning skills, and by contributing to student knowledge, skills, and abilities. Teaching scholars also can make a significant scholarly contribution by communicating pedagogical innovations and curricular developments to peers who adopt the approaches.

6. *Consistently Ethical Behavior.* Scholars should conduct their work with honesty, integrity, and objectivity. They should foster a respectful relationship with students, community participants, peers, and others who participate in or benefit from their work. Faculty standards for academic integrity represent a code of ethical behavior. For example, ethical behavior includes following the human subject review process in conducting research projects and properly crediting sources of information in writing reports, articles, and books.

Figure 11.3 *Continued*

The criteria for the "Quality and significance of scholarship" that faculty must demonstrate in their dossier followed Boyer's work:

1. Clarity and relevance of goals

2. Mastery of existing knowledge

3. Appropriate use of methodology and resources

4. Effectiveness of communication

5. Significance of results

6. Consistently ethical behavior

At the time PSU's P&T guidelines were considered revolutionary because they used Boyer's definition of scholarship, which went beyond rewarding only the scholarship related to research and added the scholarship of teaching and outreach (community-based work and service).

Dannelle read the guidelines and they seemed to make sense. She knew better than to create a laundry list of all the things she had done without an overarching organization, but wondered how she was to reconfigure her work as a school-university partnerships coordinator (two-thirds of her load) and teaching (one-third of her load) into a coherent narrative that also included "evidence" of her experience. As she read and reread the section relating to "Quality and Significance of Scholarship" (Figure 11.3), the idea that this could be configured into a scoring guide rubric jumped out at her. She took the original wording from the P&T Guidelines and separated it into descriptions of research, service, and teaching scholarship, and then put it on a grid. Figure 11.4 is what she came up with.

She put Boyer's criteria in the first column on the left. Then she separated the descriptors of these criteria, just as they were written in the PSU guidelines (Figure 11.3), into three columns, the "Expressions of scholarship: as in research, as in community outreach, as in teaching." The most important part of the process of reconfiguring the P&T guidelines was that the wording on the rubric was the exact wording found in the P&T guidelines. That lent credibility to her reconfiguration of the words. Because this is a scoring guide rubric, there are no levels of performance, only the description of the highest level of performance.

Once it was all laid out, she found it relatively simple to provide her own evidence of performance in each critical area, and so move from the rubric to the narrative. Thus, Figure 11.5, "Evidence of scholarly work in each of the dimensions of Boyer's definition of scholarship," was born and included in her dossier.

She used the specific examples from her work to show that she met the criteria within each dimension across all expressions of scholarship. She still had to write a narrative describing her work and

Expressions of Scholarship

Criteria for scholarship (Boyer, 1990)	As applied to Research	As applied to Community Outreach	As applied to Teaching
1. Clarity and relevance of goals Clearly define objectives. Clearly state basis of inquiry. Clarity of purpose	Research should address substantive intellectual, aesthetic, or creative problems or issues within one's chosen discipline. Clear objectives are necessary for fair evaluation.	Community outreach should address substantive intellectual, aesthetic, or creative problems or issues within one's chosen discipline. Clear objectives are necessary for fair evaluation.	Teaching activities are usually related to learning objectives that are appropriate within the context of curricular goals and the state of knowledge of the subject matter.
2. Mastery of existing knowledge Be well-prepared. Knowledgeable Ability to educate others Conduct research.	Propose methodologies, measures, and interventions that reflect theory, conceptualizations, and cumulative wisdom.	Propose methodologies, measures, and interventions that reflect theory, conceptualizations, and cumulative wisdom.	Demonstrate a command of resources and exhibit a depth, breadth, and understanding of subject and respond to student learning needs and evaluate teaching and curricular innovation.
3. Appropriate use of methodology and resources Address goals with carefully constructed logic and methodology.	Rigorous research requires well-constructed methodology that allows one to determine the efficacy of tested hypotheses or chosen intervention.	Rigorous applied problem solving requires well-constructed methodology that allows one to determine the efficacy of tested hypotheses or chosen intervention.	Apply appropriate pedagogy and instructional techniques to maximize student learning and use appropriate methodology to evaluate the effectiveness of curricular activities.
4. Effectiveness of communication: oral and written Convert knowledge into language that public can understand.	Make formal presentations and write effective manuscripts or reports . . . that meet professional standards of intended audience.	Make formal presentations and write effective manuscripts or reports . . . that meet professional standards of intended audience.	Communicate in ways that build positive student rapport and clarify new knowledge so as to facilitate learning. Disseminate the results of curricular innovations to teaching peers.
5. Significance of results Peers and other multiple and credible sources evaluate significance of results.	Disseminate their work to invite scrutiny and to measure degrees of critical acclaim. Consider more than direct user satisfaction.	Make a difference in communities and beyond by defining or resolving relevant social problems, facilitating organizational development, improving practices or programs, or enriching the cultural life of the community. Widely disseminate to share with others who don't directly benefit.	Make a difference in students' lives by raising motivation to learn, by developing lifelong learning skills, and by contributing to knowledge, skills, and abilities. Make a significant scholarly contribution by communicating pedagogical innovations.
6. Consistently ethical behavior	Conduct work with honesty, integrity, and objectivity. Foster a respectful relationship with students, community participants, peers, and others who participate in or benefit from their work. Faculty standards for academic integrity represent a code of ethical behavior. Includes following the human subject review process . . . and properly crediting sources of information in writing reports, articles, and books.		

Figure 11.4 Dannelle's rubric derived from Portland State 1994 (revised 2006) Promotion and Tenure Guidelines, pp. 6–7.

Evidence of Expressions of Scholarship

Criteria for scholarship (Boyer, 1990)	As applied to Research	As applied to Community Outreach	As applied to Teaching
1. Clarity and relevance of goals Clearly define objectives. Clearly state basis of inquiry. Clarity of purpose	Goals and objectives of research described in research proposals to Institutional Review Board and in paper presentations and publications.	List of meetings with school districts when Goals 2000 projects were collaboratively planned. Copy of application given to school districts to invite them to be partners for professional development with Portland State.	Syllabi from 3 core classes taught over the last 5 years. Highlight course objectives linked to National Teaching Board standards and Master's program goals and objectives and then to course assessments (assignments).
2. Mastery of existing knowledge Be well-prepared. Knowledgeable Ability to educate others Conduct research.	Literature reviews included in articles published. See Stevens & Everhart, 1997, article on school-university partnerships for sample of literature review.	Positive responses of reviewers to my conference proposals and papers about adequacy of literature review List of workshops invited to present on building partnerships	Participated in 5 professional development workshops at conferences to keep current with changes in teaching and research
3. Appropriate use of methodology and resources Address goals with carefully constructed logic and methodology.	Clearly identify the purposes of my research in my paper presentations and journal articles.	List of 20 Goals 2000 action research workshops presented in 15 area school districts over 3 years	Used rubrics to assess student learning. Matched rubrics to student course outcomes and reflected on effectiveness.
4. Effectiveness of communication: oral and written Convert knowledge into language that public can understand.	Papers written and accepted by 3 journals. Reviewer for action research special interest group for American Educational Research Association	Letters of support from 4 principals in school districts where our Professional Development Partnerships have been created Copies of "Graduate School of Education PDP newsletter" published 8 times over 3 years	Analysis of student evaluation forms, especially the items that relate to student perception that they have learned something
5. Significance of results Peers and other multiple and credible sources evaluate significance of results.	4 citations in Social Science Citation Index 15 paper presentations 6 publications while at PSU 1 edited volume written and in publication	Six schools became Professional Development Project sites for the Graduate School of Education. Student teachers placed at schools; faculty members deliver professional development activities	Reflection on the analysis of the student evaluation forms, identifying those things that get high scores and identifying those that get low scores
6. Consistently ethical behavior	All research approved by the Human Subjects and Institutional Review Board, Portland State. Chair and committee member of the committee on the role and status of women for American Educational Research Association for 4 years.		

Figure 11.5 Derived from the Portland State University Guidelines for Promotion and Tenure, 1994, 2006. Evidence provided that shows Dannelle's work meets the criteria within each "expression" of scholarship: research, outreach, and teaching.

showing how it was scholarship in each category. However, when she wrote it, she had the reference points provided by Boyer's criteria for scholarship as applied to the expressions of scholarship. Her final narrative was organized into the three typical sections—research, teaching, and outreach (service)—but within each section she wrote about each of the criteria going down the left-hand side of the rubric as applied to her work as a school-university partnerships coordinator and to demonstrate the scholarship embedded in her work.

She got tenure and, later, promotion to full professor using the same scoring guide to organize her scholarly contributions.

Conclusion

Using rubrics can help faculty members reflect on their work, write narratives for themselves and external audiences, consider perspectives they may not have thought of before, evaluate their progress, and affirm what they are already doing. Reflecting on these rubrics helps to give us the language we need to talk about and write about our work to external audiences.

Writing narratives for job applications, annual review, tenure, and promotion not only meets external expectations but also encourages professors to reflect carefully and critically on what they do. Stephen Brookfield (1995), a noted scholar of adult learning through critical reflection, urges us to critically reflect on what we do as teachers.

> The critically reflective habit confers a deeper benefit than that of a procedural utility. It embeds not only our actions but also our sense of who we are as teachers in an examined reality. We know why we believe what we believe. A critically reflective teacher is much better placed to communicate to colleagues and students—as well as to herself—the rationale behind her practice. She works from a position of informed commitment. She knows why she does what she does, why she thinks what she thinks. Knowing this, she communicates to students a confidence-inducing sense of being grounded. This sense of groundedness stabilizes her when she feels swept along by forces she cannot control . . . A critical rationale for

practice is a psychological, professional and political necessity . . . A rationale serves as a methodological and ethical
touchstone. (p. 23)

This chapter has focused on the use of certain rubrics and the narratives they generate in terms of career advancement. As Brookfield
notes, it is important to remember that these narratives are powerful
statements of who we are personally and professionally. The rubrics
in this chapter can provide a solid framework for critical reflection on
our practice and developing these narratives.

12

RUBRICS AND PROGRAM ASSESSMENT

Want to know how to clear an entire building of faculty offices in less than two minutes? No, it has nothing to do with smashing glass, pulling a handle, or yelling, "Fire!" Simply murmur the words "program assessment," and watch as the halls and offices empty. For many faculty members, those two words bring up stress-filled memories of hours of paperwork; even more hours of pointless, conflict-ridden meetings; and at the end of it all, a report that bears almost no resemblance to what they do, what they want to do daily, and what real difference it might make in student learning. Program assessment doesn't have to be like that. It isn't always like that, but we all remember cases when it has been.

Program assessments are usually carried out for three basic reasons:

- Annual departmental review: as part of a regular (often annual) form of self-assessment, usually by departments for their own information.
- Annual departmental accountability for others: as a more formal accountability review in which the criteria are set by the department under review but with the understanding that the results will be shared with others.
- Accreditation review: as part of an accreditation review in which other entities determine the criteria to be assessed and evaluated.

Rubrics are most useful in the first two instances where both their creation and their use becomes part of the daily life of the program being assessed. In accreditation reviews, and in other cases where the process is more hierarchical, rubrics are less effective, especially if the faculty themselves did not design the rubrics; however, they can still help clarify, ease, and control the process.

Rubrics can make the difference between turning the assessment experience into a waste of time, and making it a positive and enriching experience for all involved. Using rubrics created by those with a stake in the program being assessed also begins a much-needed process in changing how assessment is carried out, presented, and acted on. Rubrics can also make a major change in the culture of academic assessment to ensure that programs are assessed according to the goals and program objectives that faculty created and care about.

In this chapter, we look at three forms of program assessment in which rubrics are used: Walvoord's (2010) basic, "no-frills" departmental assessment; Portland State's University Studies "frills-included" program assessment using student work; and a "fully frilled" national rubric for program assessment, the VALUE rubrics from American Association of Colleges and Universities.

The Walvoord Basic, "No-Frills" Department Assessment Method

Walvoord (2010) recommends that departments implement an annual review of their goals and progress toward those goals using a four-hour "no-frills" method. Her method involves setting learning goals (see Appendix B for assistance in writing learning goals and student learning outcomes) for all degrees, certificates, or programs the department offers, and then using two measures to determine how well students are or are not achieving all goals or one particular goal of interest to the department. She recommends two measures: a direct measure in which faculty analyze student work and an indirect measure involving surveys or student focus groups. The results of these measures are then discussed during a four-hour department meeting that not only evaluates overall student learning results, but also decides on one action to take to improve student learning. The results of that meeting are preserved through the minutes.

Walvoord (2010) illustrates her "no-frills" method with a case study involving a biology department that featured a capstone class in which undergraduates completed a research project and wrote the results in a scientific report format. The instructor grading these reports used a rubric. The department, in turn, used that rubric to conduct a no-frills assessment of its capstone class and, by extension, of its majors'

Case Study 2: A Rubric-Based Faculty Evaluation of Student Work

At a teaching institution with no graduate degrees in biology, the department had a capstone course called "Biological Research" in which students completed a major scientific research project and wrote up their work in scientific report format.	To evaluate student research reports, the instructor developed a rubric. The department instituted the annual meeting. At the meeting, the capstone teacher reported students' strengths and weaknesses, using rubric scores (Table 3.1).

Table 3.1   Class Average Rubric Scores for Science Reports

Trait	Average scores for class in Year 1	Average scores for class in Year 2
Title	2.95	3.22
Introduction	3.18	3.64
Scientific format	3.09	3.32
Methods and materials	3.00	3.55
Non-experimental information	3.18	3.50
Designing the experiment	2.68	3.32
Defining operationally	2.68	3.50
Controlling variables	2.73	3.18
Collecting data	2.86	3.36
Interpreting data	2.90	3.59
Overall	2.93	3.42

Figure 12.1   Walvoord's table used for case study for "no-frills" program assessment. Source: Walvoord & Anderson, 2010, p. 167. Used with permission, John Wiley publisher.

learning experience, by comparing scores on individual dimensions (traits) over a two-year period (see Figure 12.1). The department meets for four hours at the beginning of the year to plan what direct and indirect data to collect. The next year they analyze the data collected.

That simple comparison quickly alerted the department that their two lowest-scoring items were "Designing the Experiment" and "Controlling Variables." The department decided to focus on "Designing the Experiment" and assigned an ad hoc committee to examine the curriculum and talk with focus groups of students. The committee determined that students generally understood the theory of experimental design, but they often failed to practice it because they saw their own labs as exercises in following a recipe and producing correct answers to teacher-generated questions. The department recommended a series of brown bag lunches to discuss how to change teaching methods in the labs.

Walvoord further suggests that each department that uses the no-frills method post a 2- or 3-page description of its assessment system on an institutional site so it can be used for other reviews and for accreditation. The description can be a compilation of the minutes of the meetings and the actions taken. Certainly, rubric data are not the only data departments can consider for program or department assessment. Yet the inherent consistency of standards on the rubrics and the relationship of rubrics to program outcomes make students' work based on the rubric a valuable source of information about program outcomes for department members.

Portland State's University Studies "Frills-Included" Annual Assessment

One annual review that takes Walvoord's "no-frills" review, adds a few frills, and expands the entire process is that implemented every year by the University Studies program at Portland State University. The University Studies program offers the freshman core, Freshman Inquiry, better known as FRINQ, a program of one-year, interdisciplinary classes organized around different themes such as "Forbidden Knowledge" or "Sustainability, Power, and Imagination." These classes are team-taught not only on the Portland State campus, but also in community colleges and even as part of some high school Advanced Placement (AP) offerings. Portland State is an urban campus with a very diverse student population, and FRINQ ensures that all incoming freshmen have the skills needed to succeed in higher education, and introduces these students to the opportunities the university experience affords them. This is an ambitious and somewhat amorphous goal that inevitably gives rise to the question: Is it working?

To determine that, the University Studies faculty developed the Four Goals of University Studies: Inquiry and Critical Thinking,

Communication, The Diversity of Human Experience, and Ethics and Social Responsibility (Brown, 2005). The faculty then developed six-level, holistic rubrics to be used in assessing how well the program was or was not meeting these goals. Initially, there were four such rubrics, but after the assessment program had been in effect for several years, it was decided that the Communication rubric was too general and needed to be subdivided further into written communication and quantitative literacy; that was done and separate rubrics were created accordingly (Carpenter, 2010). (The full set of rubrics can be found in Appendices E–I; they are also available for download in Word or PDF at http://pdx.edu/unst/university-studies-goals.)

Those new rubrics, like the ones before them, were created primarily by the faculty who teach in FRINQ and who are intimately acquainted with the goals being assessed. That part of the process is perhaps as important as the assessment itself. Involving the faculty so extensively ensures that the rubrics are actually relevant to the goals and allows for changes that naturally occur over time as a result of real, in-class experiences. The Communications rubrics are not the only examples of such changes. Faculty committees periodically reexamine and revise all of the University Studies rubrics. This also has the added benefit of reminding the faculty about what they are trying to accomplish in their classes. Some faculty feel that the experience of drawing and redrawing the rubrics is at least as valuable as analyzing student scores on their final products using the rubrics.

The student final products, however, are what are used in the actual assessment process that occurs at the end of each school year. The process begins with collecting random student portfolios, three from each FRINQ class, resulting in an average of 200 or more portfolios. These portfolios are created by the students and structured around the Four Goals of University Studies. They represent the work each student has done over the course of the year, and each student's own commentary on how well (or badly) the work reveals his or her achievements in each goal. In the early days of FRINQ, these portfolios were massive volumes constituting examples of student work for each of the four University Studies goals, along with student reflections on the work, and the whole amounted to a daunting display of work to be done. These days, they are almost all e-portfolios that look far less daunting and require no heavy lifting.

Regardless of the form, however, the resulting collection of portfolios goes far beyond the ability of the University Studies faculty to assess on their own. To do that requires a 2- to 3-day effort involving 40–50 reviewers drawn from as many departments and disciplines as possible. This is not just a practical necessity, although it is true that there are too few University Studies faculty to handle the task; it is also a choice. The aim is make the faculty generally more aware of the goals of University Studies and to offer greater transparency for the program (Carpenter, 2010).

These reviewers receive preliminary training in the use of the rubrics and are then set to work to assess each student portfolio according to the five rubrics provided. Each student portfolio is assessed by two evaluators. In cases where those assessments are seriously at odds, a third evaluator is brought in and a final evaluation is determined (Carpenter, 2010).

The evaluations are then compiled and the results discussed at a fall retreat. They are reviewed further by each team working separately. Teams use the data to determine which goal is the weakest in actual achievement, and they devise a plan to improve student learning outcomes in the following year. There are no specific rules regarding what such a plan should entail, but they usually involve some sort of shared assignment, exercise, or reading related to the selected goal. (FRINQ team-teaching focuses on a shared theme, but each faculty member retains considerable autonomy regarding readings and assignments.)

The annual assessment and the intense faculty involvement create a remarkably detailed record of student learning outcomes over time and timely feedback that is of immediate use to the faculty. The fact that faculty create and use the rubrics involved in the assessment and use those same rubrics unites the otherwise diverse FRINQ faculty and ensures that they are actually being assessed on what they are trying to accomplish. Such an assessment process is an excellent case study of what it means to create a system of assessment by the faculty, for the faculty, and of the faculty (Levi & Stevens, 2010; Rhodes, 2010).

The VALUE Rubrics "All-Frills-Inclusive" Assessment Package

Most departments and programs, however, cannot afford to create and maintain a massive rubrics-based, continuing system of assessment such as the one FRINQ uses. And even committed departments may find it difficult to manage any form of overarching rubrics for all of their class offerings. Note that Walvoord's "no-frills" case study involved using a classroom rubric developed by one of the faculty, not a rubric developed by the entire department, to measure overall program goals. And not all departments will have the advantage of having a faculty member who uses such a rubric and is willing to share it, and it is one that matches program outcomes. To help with that situation, the Association of American Colleges and Universities has created the Valid Assessment of Learning in Undergraduate Education (VALUE), a set of United States national rubrics that offers models of assessment to any university interested in using rubrics to measure a variety of outcomes and for any form of assessment (Adler-Kassner, Rutz, & Harrington, 2010).

The VALUE rubrics are the work of over 100 faculty members across the United States and other experts who worked in teams to produce 15 rubrics in three categories.

Intellectual and Practical Skills

- Inquiry and analysis
- Critical thinking
- Creative thinking
- Written communication
- Oral communication
- Reading
- Quantitative
- Literacy
- Information literacy
- Teamwork
- Problem solving

Personal and Social Responsibility

- Civic engagement
- Intercultural knowledge and competence
- Ethical reasoning
- Foundations and skills for lifelong learning

Integrative and Applied Learning

- Integrative and applied learning (Morgaine, 2010; Rhodes, 2010; www.aacu.org/value/rubric_teams.cfm)

These rubrics can be downloaded at www.aacu.org/value/rubrics/index_p.cfm–CFID = 37546491&CFTOKEN = 96625379. They are free, but you must register to access them. They are in .pdf and .doc (revisable) formats.

Because they were produced by faculty members, the VALUE rubrics reflect the shared language of academe and can be used as is in some cases, but this is not what they are designed for. Instead, they are intended to be models, to provide the basic language and a beginning outline faculty members can use to create their own assessment rubrics. Indeed, the Association of American Colleges and Universities recommends that they "can and should be translated into the language of individual campuses, disciplines, and even courses" (Rhodes, 2010, p. 21). We recommend using an adapted version of the method outlined in Chapter 7 on "Making It Yours."

Rules for Good Program Assessment Using Rubrics

Designing program assessment rubrics requires participation of many faculty and administrators who work in the program. There are several rules to keep in mind to guide the development of successful and representative program rubrics.

1. The best program assessments use rubrics and other criteria that are developed primarily by those involved in the program who are best acquainted with the goals and values of the program.

2. Although some faculty members inevitably will be more enthusiastic and engaged than others, everyone should participate to some degree. This not only builds community and shared values, but faculty who use rubrics for assessment are more likely to use them for classroom grading as well.

3. Creating rubrics for assessment is an ongoing process. Thus, first drafts and even later versions should be viewed as works in progress and approached with the understanding that changes, sometimes very substantial, are possible and often desirable (Morgaine, 2010).

4. Remember that program assessment is about assessing programs, not individuals. Individual assessments of faculty should be entirely separate. Faculty members should be informed of this focus.

5. Rubrics are best suited to assessing direct materials such as student portfolios, papers, and other assignments.

6. Grades alone are not adequate for program assessment because they do not contain enough information about the strengths and weaknesses of the program.

7. All program assessment should be followed by action, for the sake of improvement and to ensure that the assessment process remains meaningful to those who participate in it.

EPILOGUE:
THE RUBRICS MANIFESTO

At their core, rubrics are part of a major shift, a major redistribution of power, in how academe defines and controls education. That redistribution of power begins in the classroom where professors use rubrics to give their students the power of access, to allow them to better understand what is expected of them, and to contribute to those expectations in ways that give them a greater stake in their own learning. It continues on an individual level to the faculty who use rubrics to document and define their progress in their fields. And it becomes systemic when departments, programs, and even entire campuses use rubrics to define their shared goals and to document how well they are doing in them. That redistribution is long overdue on all levels.

For students, especially nontraditional students, rubrics are a guide to the culture and language of academe, a culture and language with which many of them are unacquainted, and of which many are not fully conscious. When they are involved in rubric creation, even at a very minimal level such the Presentation and Feedback Model described in Chapter 4, they begin to understand that "learning" is an active verb, that there is a vocabulary that defines *progress in learning*, and that they can and should play a role in defining and furthering a learning environment on their own campuses. Simply knowing that makes students stakeholders in their own college careers. It also offers them insights into what they can and cannot expect from higher education, and understanding about how and why a university degree differs from a vocational certificate.

For faculty members who use rubrics in their classrooms and to chart their own progress in teaching, research, and other career-related activities, the same is true. They, too, discover that rubrics can give them greater control to define and document their own achievements and to become greater stakeholders in their own campus lives.

That has obvious benefits for their own promotion and tenure prospects, but it is also a way for even very new faculty to become involved in defining and redefining the goals and progress of their individual institutions. Indeed, their classroom rubrics, and even sometimes their personal assessment rubrics, can form the basis for larger discussions of teaching goals, promotion and tenure guidelines, and even assessment efforts, as shown in Walvoord's basic, "no-frills" model described in Chapter 12.

For departments, programs, and even entire universities, using rubrics for assessment at all levels not only can improve performance, but also can document it. That in itself is a major step in empowering faculty to take greater control of how higher education is defined, structured, and often restructured. Taking such control has never been more urgent. Defining and judging higher education is all too often done by outside forces: political interests, the purveyors of college guides and ratings manuals, the media, accreditation committees, and sometimes even an emerging culture of academic administration that is increasingly disconnected from the twin pillars of academe: teaching and research. By using rubrics to define what their actual goals are and provide a model for how their progress can be assessed, faculty can exert considerable control and can produce assessment results that are more useful to them.

Administrators can play a role by facilitating such activities, but ultimately, the content of assessment rubrics must come from faculty themselves. Like mission statement reviews, the very activity of discussing what does and what does not belong on assessment rubrics has value in itself as well as in the documents it ultimately produces. It increases the stakeholder sense among the faculty and leads toward a greater understanding of what is shared even among widely divergent departments and disciplines. It will also highlight what is unique about each campus. Assessment rubrics devised for a small, religion-based, liberal arts campus are bound to differ in significant ways from those devised for a large public university. And they should.

What is surprising is not that they differ, but that they share so many of the same values. That is apparent in the VALUE rubrics described in Chapter 12. Some universities may stress some of these skills more than others. Some may leave out a few. But most will agree on basic validity of learning goals such as inquiry and analysis, critical and creative thinking, written and oral communication, quantitative literacy, and information literacy (Rhodes, 2010). The VALUE rubrics, perhaps more than anything else done to date, reveal clearly and succinctly that academe still exists and that despite massive changes and wildly increasing diversity in student populations and types of campuses, it still has a shared vision.

That is not too surprising. Rubrics come from the very foundation of academe: the classroom and the teaching experience. They reflect values that are intrinsic to academe and to education generally, but values that are too seldom articulated and defended. Rubrics are one way in which students and faculty become more aware of what those shared values are, and this gives them greater ability to share that vision with society at large, a society that is often increasingly suspicious of the value of higher education, and education generally. Faculty members, university graduates, and even many undergraduates understand what those values are and can defend them, but first they need to articulate them for themselves. Rubrics can and do play an important role in doing so.

Is this making too great a claim for the value of the humble rubric? It probably is if rubrics are considered in a vacuum, but taken in context with other efforts and evolving social phenomena, rubrics are an important part of the process of making education and the opportunities it offers more accessible and understandable to our students, ourselves, and society at large.

Adler-Kassner, L., Rutz, C., & Harrington, S. (2010). A guide for how faculty can get started using the VALUE rubrics. In T. L. Rhodes (Ed.), *Assessing outcomes and improving achievement: Tips and tools for using rubrics* (pp. 19–20). Washington, DC: Association of American Colleges and Universities.

American Council of Teachers of Foreign Languages. (1986). *ACTFL Proficiency Guidelines*. Hastings-on-the-Hudson, NY: American Council of Teachers of Foreign Languages.

American Council on Education. (September 10, 2001). Largest, most diverse freshman class enters college this fall. *Higher Education and National Affairs, 50*(16). www.acenet.edu/hena/issues/2001/09-10-01/sat.cfm

Anaya, G., & Cole, D. G. (2001). Latina/o student achievement: Exploring the influence of student-faculty interactions on college grades. *Journal of Student Development, 42*(1), 3–14.

Anderson, R. S. (1998, Summer). Why talk about different ways to grade? The shift from traditional assessment to alternative assessment. *New Directions for Teaching and Learning, 74,* 5–16.

Bernstein, D. J., Addison, W., Altman, C., Hollister, D., Komarraju, M., Prieto, L., Rocheleau, C.A., & Shore, C. (2009). Toward a scientist-educator model of teaching psychology. In D. F. Halpern (Ed.), *Undergraduate education in psychology: A blueprint for the future of the discipline* (pp. 29–45). Washington, DC: American Psychological Association.

Black, P., & Wiliam, D. (1998). Assessment and classroom learning. *Assessment in Education: Principles, Policy & Practice, 5*(1), 46 pages.

Boud, D. (1990). Assessment and the promotion of academic values. *Studies in Higher Education, 15*(1), 1–10.

Boyer, W. H. (1990). *Scholarship reconsidered: Priorities for the new century.* Princeton, NJ: Carnegie Foundation for the Advancement of Teaching.

Brinko, K. T. (1993). The practice of giving feedback. *Journal of Higher Education, 64*(5), 575–593.

Brookfield, S. (1990). *The skillful teacher: On technique, trust and skillfulness in the classroom.* San Francisco: Jossey-Bass.

Brookfield, S. D. (1995). *Becoming a critically reflective teacher.* San Francisco: Jossey-Bass.

Brown, C. L. (2005). Varying realities of the human experience: University Studies Program at Portland State University. In E. Lardner, E. (Ed.), *Diversity, educational equity & learning communities* (pp. 93–106). Olympia, WA: The Evergreen College, Washington Center for Improving the Quality of Undergraduate Education.

Caffarella, R. S., & Clark, M. C. (1999, Winter). Development and learning: Themes and conclusions. *New Directions for Adult & Continuing Education, 84,* 97–101.

Capsi, A., & Blau, I. (2008). Social presence in online discussion groups: Testing three conceptions and their relations to perceived learning. *Social Psychological Education, 11*(3), 323–346.

Carpenter, R. (2010). How do I use rubrics to evaluate student work? In T. L. Rhodes (Ed.), *Assessing outcomes and improving achievement: Tips and tools for using rubrics* (pp. 15–17). Washington DC: Association of American Colleges and Universities. Retrieved from http://www.aacu .org/bringing_theory/newsletter/jan11/faculty.cf m

College of Education, University of Central Florida. (1997). *What is a WebCamp? Guidelines for final project, Final project rubric.* www.itrc.ucf.edu/webcamp/rubrics.html

Gotcher, L. (1997). *Assessment rubrics.* http://129.7.160.115/COURSE/ INST_5931A/Rubric.html#User.

Huba, M. E., & Freed, J. E. (2000). *Learner-centered assessment on college campuses: Shifting the focus from teaching to learning.* Boston: Allyn & Bacon.

Ilgen, D. R., Peterson, R. B., Martin, B. A., & Boeschen, D. A. (1981). Supervisor and subordinate reactions to performance appraisal sessions. *Organizational Behavior & Human Performance, 28*(3), 311–331.

Kaplan, M., Meizlish, D. S., O'Neal, C., & Wright, M. C. (2008). A research-based rubric for developing statements of teaching philosophy. In D. R. Robertson & L. B. Nilson (Eds.), *To improve the academy: Resources for faculty, instructional and organizational development,* Vol. 26 (pp. 242–262*).* San Francisco: Jossey-Bass.

Kearsley, G. (2000). *Teaching and learning in cyberspace.* Toronto: Nelson Thompson Learning.

Kezar, A. (2011). *Engaged students require engaged faculty: Facing the paradox of a largely non-tenure-track faculty.* Washington, DC: American Association of Colleges and Universities. Retrieved January 3, 2011, from http://www.aacu.org/bringing_theory/newsletter/jan11/ faculty.cf m

King, P. M., & Kitchener, K. S. (1994). *Developing reflective judgment: Understanding & promoting intellectual growth and critical thinking in adolescents & adults.* San Francisco: Jossey-Bass.

Leamnson, R. N. (2002). It's never too late: Developing cognitive skills for lifelong learning. *Interactive Learning Environments, 10*(2), 93–104.

Lehman, R. M., & Conceição, S. C. O. (2010). *Creating a sense of presence in online teaching: How to "be there" for distance learners.* San Francisco: Jossey-Bass.

Levi, A. J., & Stevens, D. D. (2010). Assessment of the Academy, for the Academy, by the Academy. In T. L. Rhodes (Ed.), *Assessing outcomes and improving achievement: Tips and tools for using rubrics* (pp. 5–7). Washington, DC: Association of American Colleges and Universities.

Lewis, R., Berghoff, P., & Pheeney, P. (1999). Focusing students: Three approaches for learning through evaluation. *Innovative Higher Education, 23*(3), 181–196.

Light, R. J. (2001). *Making the most of college: Students speak their minds.* Cambridge: Harvard University Press.

Meizlish, D., & Kaplan, M. (2008). Valuing and evaluating teaching in academic hiring: A multidisciplinary, cross-institutional study. *Journal of Higher Education, 79*(5), 489–512.

Mellow, G. O., Van Slyck, P., & Enyon, B. (2002). The face of the future. *Change, 35*(2), 1–13.

Moon, J. M. (1999). *Reflection in Learning and Professional Development.* London: Kogan Page.

Morgaine, W. (2010). Developing rubrics: Lessons learned. In T. L. Rhodes (Ed.), *Assessing outcomes and improving achievement: Tips and tools for using rubrics* (pp. 11–13). Washington, DC: Association of American Colleges and Universities.

National Center for Education Statistics. (2002). Postsecondary persistence and progress: High school academic preparation and postsecondary progress (Indicator No. 23). *The Condition of Education Report.* Washington, DC: U.S. Department of Education.

NSF Synthesis Engineering Education Coalition. (1997). *Assessment tool: Design project report* (F. McMartin, Ed.). Berkeley, CA: College of Engineering, University of California, Berkeley.

Perry, W. G., Jr. (1970). *Forms of intellectual and ethical development in the college years: A scheme.* Troy, MO: Holt, Rinehart & Winston.

Portland State University (1994, 2006). Promotion and Tenure Guidelines. Portland, OR: Portland State University. Retrieved from http://www.pdx.edu/oaa/promotion-tenure-guidelines

Redder, J. (2003). *Assessing Critical Thinking in Higher Education: A Study of Rater Reliability.* Paper presented at the annual meeting of the Association for the Study of Higher Education, Portland, Oregon.

Rhodes, T. L. (2010). Introduction. In T. L. Rhodes (Ed.), *Assessing outcomes and improving achievement: Tips and tools for using rubrics* (pp. 1–3). Washington, DC: Association of American Colleges and Universities.

Rodriguez, S. (2003). What helps some first generation students succeed. *About Campus, 8*(4), 17–23.

Rucker, M. L., & Thomson, S., (2003). Assessing student learning outcomes: An investigation of the relationship among feedback measures. *College Student Journal, 37*(3), 400–405.

Schönwetter, D. J., Taylor, L., & Ellis, D. E. (2006). Reading the want ads: How can current job descriptions inform professional development programs for graduate students? *Journal on Excellence in College Teaching, 17*(1 & 2), 159–188.

Stevens, D. D., & Cooper, J. E. (2009). *Journal keeping: How to use reflective writing for learning, teaching, professional insight and positive change.* Sterling, VA: Stylus.

Stevens, D. D., & Everhart, R. E. (2000). Designing and tailoring school-university partnerships: A straightjacket, security blanket or just a loose coat? *The Professional Educator, 22*(2), 39–49.

Taras, M. (2003). To feedback or not to feedback in student self-assessment. *Assessment and Evaluation in Higher Education, 28*(5), 549–566.

Walvoord, B. E. (2010). *Assessment: Clear and simple: A practical guide for institutions, departments and general education* (2nd ed.). San Francisco: Jossey-Bass.

Walvoord, B. E., & Anderson, V. J. (2010). *Effective grading: A tool for learning and assessment in college* (2nd ed.). San Francisco: John Wiley.

Webster's Unabridged Dictionary. (1913). www.bootlegbooks.com/Reference/Webster/data/1336.html

WordNet. (1997). www.cogsci.princeton.edu/~wn/wn2.0

APPENDICES

A. Mini-Lesson 1: Writing a Task Description

B. Mini-Lesson 2: Writing Student Learning Outcomes (SLOs)

C. Blank Rubric Format for a Four-Level Rubric, Landscape Format

D. Blank Rubric Format for a Scoring Guide Rubric

E. Portland State University Studies Program Rubric: Ethical Issues

F. Portland State University Studies Program Rubric: Holistic Critical Thinking

G. Portland State University Studies Program Rubric: Quantitative Literacy

H. Portland State University Studies Program Rubric: Writing

I. Portland State University Studies Program Rubric: Diversity

J. Website Information for *Introduction to Rubrics*

MINI-LESSON 1: WRITING A TASK DESCRIPTION

A task description, which tells students about your course assignment, is a distillation of what should be spelled out more fully in the rubric. When you pass out the syllabus on the first day of class, students do not read your well-crafted course introduction or your clear student learning outcomes; instead, they flip to the page that describes the assignments. They are already calculating how much time and effort they will have to devote to this class. Therefore, it is very important that you pay attention to how you describe the assignment. This will be helpful to them and certainly helpful to you because you will spend less time describing it in class and addressing questions during office hours. A clear task description in the syllabus, accompanied by a rubric that has the task description on the top of the page, will solve many problems way ahead of time.

Elements in an Excellent Task Description

Descriptive title for the assignment: Not "term paper" but "action research literature review," "argumentative essay," or "creative brief"

Purpose: Write a sentence about why you want students to do this assignment and how it fits in with the course objectives. Think about: Why am I assigning this paper? What is its purpose? What do I want students to learn or demonstrate by doing this assignment?

Definitions: Provide a clear definition of any key terms that students may not be familiar with. For example, "A literature review is . . ."

Support: Describe how you will help students complete the assignment successfully. How will you support their development of the paper or project? Will you allow drafts? Can they turn in sections of the paper before the final paper or project is due?

Scope: These are the details. What will the final product look like? What is the length (a constant student question)? Is it graded by points or percentages? Due dates? Format? Presentation—folder, stapled, binder, etc.? The rubric dimension descriptions, such as "conventions," can provide more details, including pages numbered, correct grammar, correct citation format, etc. (See Figure 10.1, Horton's literature review rubric.)

Here is an example of a **weak task description:**

Assignment: *Term paper: All students are expected to write a term paper, selecting a topic from the themes presented each week. It is due the last day of class.*

Here is an example of a **better task description:**

Assignment: *Action research literature review: You will write a literature review to acquaint you with additional resources to help you think about and conduct your action research project. A literature review is a summary of research others have done on the topic that you identified in the problem statement. You will need to use the library databases to find at least 10 journal articles related to your topic. We will have two class sessions on how to summarize, analyze, and critique these journal articles. The review should be 6–10 pages. It will be turned in as a draft by the third week of class and will be returned to you for revision. Your final version is due with the other parts of your action research proposal—the problem statement and the methods—during the week before finals week. Other more detailed criteria can be found on the attached rubric. This paper is worth 15 of 100 points total for all assignments.*

MINI-LESSON 2: WRITING STUDENT LEARNING OUTCOMES (SLOs)

Learning outcomes are the centerpiece of course development. Learning outcomes guide rubric development as well. Outcomes are what you want students to know, comprehend, and be able to do when they walk out of your class. Yet, writing good clear outcomes takes time and practice. Most faculty members think of student learning outcomes in terms of the cognitive outcomes, what you want students to know. Today, many abbreviate student learning outcomes as SLOs.

Characteristics of Well-Developed Student Learning Outcomes

Written for the student not the teacher: A good learning outcome is what the **students will be able to do**, not what you are doing to help students learn. Think of student performance, not teaching activities. For example, "Discuss the chapter" is more of a teaching activity than a student outcome. Think about what you want students to learn from discussing the chapter, not the activity of discussing the chapter: "From class discussion, students will be able to state the assumptions the author makes about. . . ."

Uses active verbs: Seek to use verbs that you can see the student doing, not something taking place in their heads: NOT "understand," NOT "learn," NOT "know," NOT "appreciate." These are hard to measure and it is difficult to ascertain whether students have accomplished these outcomes. When creating SLOs for cognitive outcomes, use the verbs "write," "analyze," "evaluate," "demonstrate," "explain." These are active verbs. The following are some websites with lists of active verbs that are enormously helpful in writing student learning outcomes. Note: Most think of using the verbs associated with Bloom's Taxonomy of Cognitive Objectives for writing cognitive SLOs. There is a 20th-century original version and a twenty-first-century version. The twenty-first-century version added the outcome "Create" and modified others. You will see both on the Internet and in the following links.

Is measurable: As you create and finalize your SLOs, always be asking yourself what assignment or activity you can use to assess whether students have really accomplished this outcome. Then develop a rubric to assess how well students did in meeting the outcome.

> **Weak student learning outcome:**
> You will learn about the characteristics of a good literature review.

> **Well-developed student learning outcome:**
> (At the end of this course) Students will be able to write a literature review that synthesizes, analyzes, and critiques the research literature germane to their topic.

Links to websites with verbs and descriptions of cognitive student learning outcomes:
> www.wcu.edu/WebFiles/WordDocs/wcucfc_bloomsverbsmatrix.doc
> www.personal.psu.edu/bxb11/Objectives/ActionVerbsforObjectives.pdf
> www.odu.edu/educ/roverbau/Bloom/blooms_taxonomy.htm
> www.celt.iastate.edu/teaching/RevisedBlooms1.html

Links to websites with verbs and descriptions of noncognitive student learning outcomes such as for performances, physical skills, values, and dispositions. Sometimes these are called "psychomotor outcomes" and "affective outcomes":
> www.businessballs.com/bloomstaxonomyoflearningdomains.htm
> www.wisc-online.com/objects/ViewObject.aspx?ID = OTT402

BLANK RUBRIC FORMAT FOR A FOUR-LEVEL RUBRIC, LANDSCAPE FORMAT

Four-Level Rubric, Landscape Format

Task Description:

Dimensions	Exemplary	Accomplished	Developing	Beginning

BLANK RUBRIC FORMAT FOR A SCORING GUIDE RUBRIC

Scoring Guide Rubric

Task Description:

Dimensions	Description of highest level of performance	Comments	Points

PORTLAND STATE UNIVERSITY STUDIES PROGRAM RUBRIC: ETHICAL ISSUES

Ethical Issues and Social Responsibility

6 (highest)	Portfolio creatively and comprehensively articulates approaches to ethical issues and social responsibility in a scholarly manner, citing specific evidence. Demonstrates an ability to view multiple sides of these issues, to question what is being taught, and to construct independent meaning and interpretations.
	Portfolio presents well-developed ideas on the role of ethical issues and social responsibility in both private and public life. Demonstrates a deep awareness of how a conceptual understanding of ethical issues and social responsibility manifests concretely in one's personal choices, including decisions on when and how to act.
5	Portfolio analyzes ethical issues and social responsibility in a scholarly manner and makes thoughtful connections between this area of study and its effects on lives, ideas, and events.
	Portfolio discusses explicitly how a deepening understanding of ethical issues and social responsibility has influenced personal opinions, decisions, and views on the role of the self in society.
4	Portfolio thoughtfully analyzes, in a scholarly manner, a situation or situations in which ethical issues and social responsibility have played an important role. Begins to investigate connections between areas of controversy and to extrapolate meaning from specific examples.
	Portfolio applies learning in ethical issues and social responsibility to issues that arise in everyday life and contemplates the impact of personal ethical choices and social action in the context of interpersonal and broader societal spheres.
3	Portfolio exhibits a working knowledge of major themes and scholarly debates surrounding ethical issues and social responsibility and applies this understanding to some topics but offers no independent analysis.
	References ethical issues and social responsibility as a subject of personal inquiry, begins to question established views, and contemplates in some way the value and impact of individual choices and personal action on one's broader community.
2	Portfolio mentions some issue(s) involving ethics or talks about social responsibility in a general fashion but does not discuss these areas in a meaningful way.
	Portfolio contains some evidence of self-reflection in the area of ethical issues or social responsibility, but this reflection is superficial and reveals little or no questioning of established views.
1 (lowest)	Portfolio displays little or no engagement with the subjects of ethical issues and social responsibility.
	Demonstrates little or no recognition of ethical issues and social responsibility as subjects worthy of personal inquiry.
X =	No basis for scoring (Use only for missing or malfunctioning portfolios.)

Note: In this scoring guide, the phrase "ethical issues and social responsibility" refers to the impact and value of individuals and their choices on society—intellectually, socially, and personally.

PORTLAND STATE UNIVERSITY STUDIES PROGRAM RUBRIC: HOLISTIC CRITICAL THINKING

Inquiry and Critical Thinking Rubric

Students will learn various modes of inquiry through interdisciplinary curricula—problem posing, investigating, conceptualizing—in order to become active, self-motivated, and empowered learners.

6 (Highest)—Consistently does all or almost all of the following:

- Accurately interprets evidence, statements, graphics, questions, etc.
- Identifies the salient arguments (reasons and claims) pro and con.
- Thoughtfully analyzes and evaluates major alternative points of view.
- Generates alternative explanations of phenomena or events.
- Justifies key results and procedures; explains assumptions and reasons.
- Fair-mindedly follows where evidence and reasons lead.
- Makes ethical judgments.

5—Does most of the following:

- Accurately interprets evidence, statements, graphics, questions, etc.
- Thinks through issues by identifying relevant arguments (reasons and claims) pro and con.
- Offers analysis and evaluation of obvious alternative points of view.
- Generates alternative explanations of phenomena or events.
- Justifies (by using) some results or procedures; explains reasons.
- Fair-mindedly follows where evidence and reasons lead.

4—Does most of the following:

- Describes events, people, and places with some supporting details from the source.
- Makes connections to sources, either personal or analytic.
- Demonstrates a basic ability to analyze, interpret, and formulate inferences.
- States or briefly includes more than one perspective in discussing literature, experiences, and points of view of others.
- Takes some risks by occasionally questioning sources or by stating interpretations and predictions.
- Demonstrates little evidence of rethinking or refinement of one's own perspective.

3—Does most or many of the following:

- Responds by retelling or graphically showing events or facts.

- Makes personal connections or identifies connections within or between sources in a limited way.
- Is beginning to use appropriate evidence to back ideas.
- Discusses literature, experiences, and points of view of others in terms of own experience.
- Responds to sources at factual or literal level.
- Includes little or no evidence of refinement of initial response or shift in dualistic thinking.
- Demonstrates difficulty with organization, and thinking is uneven.

2—Does most or many of the following:

- Misinterprets evidence, statements, graphics, questions, etc.
- Fails to identify strong, relevant counterarguments.
- Draws unwarranted or fallacious conclusions.
- Justifies few results or procedures; seldom explains reasons.
- Regardless of the evidence or reasons, maintains or defends views based on self-interest or preconceptions.

1 (Lowest)—Consistently does all or almost all of the following:

- Offers biased interpretations of evidence, statements, graphics, questions, information, or the points of view of others.
- Fails to identify or hastily dismisses strong, relevant counterarguments.
- Ignores or superficially evaluates obvious alternative points of view. Argues using fallacious or irrelevant reasons and unwarranted claims.
- Does not justify results or procedures, nor explains reasons.
- Exhibits close-mindedness or hostility to reason.

X—No basis for scoring (Use only for missing or malfunctioning portfolios.)

PORTLAND STATE UNIVERSITY STUDIES PROGRAM RUBRIC: QUANTITATIVE LITERACY

The Quantitative Literacy Rubric

6. Portfolio demonstrates evidence of ability to conduct independent research and to integrate the results with other methodologies in original work. The meaning of statistical significance, calculus, a comprehensive understanding of causality and correlation, applications of normal curves and outliers to physical and social phenomena, and an integrated comprehension of linear regression is comprehensively displayed.

5. Portfolio demonstrates evidence of ability to conduct independent research and to integrate the results with other methodologies in original work, although not to the fullest extent possible. The meaning of statistical significance, a comprehensive understanding of causality and correlation, applications of normal curves and outliers to physical and social phenomena, and an integrated comprehension of linear regression is present but not fully displayed.

4. Portfolio contains assignments demonstrating evidence of an ability to read, understand, and critique books or articles that make use of quantitative reasoning, using descriptive statistics, understanding the meaning of statistical significance, and displaying data using appropriate graphs and charts. Assignments are included in the portfolio as separate entities, and quantitative reasoning is integrated into other work.

3. Portfolio demonstrates evidence of an ability to read, understand, and critique books or articles that make use of quantitative reasoning, using descriptive statistics (mean, median, mode), understanding the meaning of statistical significance, and displaying data using appropriate graphs and charts. Alternatively, well-designed and appropriate quantitative reasoning assignments are included in the portfolio but are treated as separate entities.

2. Portfolio demonstrates evidence of limited ability to define, duplicate, label, list, recognize, and reproduce mathematical and statistical elements. Portfolio displays limited or no evidence of meaningful application of these numerical concepts.

1. Portfolio demonstrates no evidence of ability to evaluate mathematics and statistics, including no knowledge of basic descriptive statistics.

PORTLAND STATE UNIVERSITY STUDIES PROGRAM RUBRIC: WRITING

Score of 6:

- The student portfolio demonstrates the ability to communicate clearly for a variety of purposes and diverse audiences.
- The portfolio shows the mark of the writer's own labor, critical judgment, and rhetorical shaping.
- It is marked by lucid and orderly thinking, substantial depth, fullness and complexity of thought.
- It articulates metacognition on the writer's part: analysis of learning strategies, revision techniques, and improvement in writing skills.
- It evidences control of diction, syntactic variety, and usage.

Score of 5:

- The student portfolio reveals the ability to communicate for a variety of purposes and diverse audiences.
- The portfolio satisfactorily shows the mark of the writer's own labor, critical judgment, and rhetorical shaping.
- The main ideas are well supported with a fair degree of specificity.
- Organization reveals clarity of thought and paragraphs are coherent units.
- The writing is largely free of errors in mechanics, usage, and sentence structure.

Score of 4:

- The portfolio does come to terms with the basic tasks of the assignments, but overall it executes the assignments less completely or less systematically than a 6 or 5 portfolio.
- There is no serious weakness in organization. Though there may be some disjointedness and lack of focus, the reader can move with relative ease through the discourse.
- Generalizations are usually supported, though some detail may be lacking or irrelevant.
- The portfolio contains some errors in sentence structure and mechanics but not to the point of distracting the reader from the content.

Score of 3:

- The student portfolio shows difficulty in managing the tasks of the assignment.
- There is likely to be either a weakness in analytical thinking or lack of development of key ideas.

- The portfolio marginally demonstrates the ability to communicate for a variety of purposes.
- Errors in sentence structure, usage, and mechanics do interfere with readability.
- Overall, the portfolio shows some metacognition on the student's part, but there is lack of clarity and depth about revising and the writing process.

Score of 2:

- The portfolio does not come to terms with the assignment.
- There is little development of ideas, and the reader finds it difficult to follow from one point to the next.
- Writing tasks may be ignored or badly mishandled.
- There may be serious errors in reasoning.
- There may be serious and frequent errors in sentence structure, usage, and mechanics.
- Overall, the portfolio reveals an inability to communicate successfully.

Score of 1:

- The portfolio reveals a combination of rhetorical problems from conceptual confusion, disorganization, and a basic inability to handle language.

PORTLAND STATE UNIVERSITY STUDIES PROGRAM RUBRIC: DIVERSITY

The Diversity of Human Experience

6 (highest)	Portfolio creatively and comprehensively demonstrates an understanding of personal, institutional, and ideological issues surrounding diversity in a scholarly fashion, using concrete examples. The work reflects an ability to view issues from multiple perspectives, to question what is being taught, and to construct independent meaning and interpretations. Demonstrates broad awareness of how the self appears from the greater perspective of human experience, questions own views in light of this awareness, and contemplates its implications for life choices in the personal and public spheres.
5	Portfolio presents persuasive arguments about, and insights into, prominent issues surrounding diversity and discusses ways in which personal and cultural experiences influence lives, ideas, and events. Reflects on personal experiences within the broader context of human experience, demonstrating a sophisticated awareness of the limitations of subjective experience and an informed view of the role difference plays in societies and institutions.
4	Portfolio analyzes some issue(s) surrounding diversity and demonstrates an ability to understand particular situations in the context of current concepts and theory. Discusses personal experience within the broader context of human experience—demonstrating a working knowledge of features of diverse peoples, societies, and institutions and analyzes these features in some way.
3	Portfolio demonstrates a basic working knowledge of central theories and concepts related to the study of diversity. Demonstrates some attempt to meaningfully locate oneself within the broader context of diverse culture.
2	Portfolio demonstrates a basic comprehension of some issues surrounding diversity but refers only in a limited way to current theory and concepts. Relates personal experiences within the context of broader human experiences but does not locate self within that context in a thoughtful manner.
1 (lowest)	Portfolio uses some terminology surrounding diversity but fails to demonstrate meaningful comprehension of key concepts. Tells of personal experiences but does not connect, compare, or contrast those with the experiences of others.

Note: In this scoring guide, "diversity" refers to differences in ethnic, religious, and cultural perspectives, class, race, gender, age, sexual orientation, and ability.

WEBSITE INFORMATION FOR
INTRODUCTION TO RUBRICS

We have created a website for

- Downloading rubrics
- Sharing rubrics
- Discussing the use of rubrics

Please feel free to contact us about rubrics and even about doing workshops with faculty on creating rubrics. The address is www.stylus
pub.com/resources/introductiontorubrics.aspx.

Also available from Stylus

Journal Keeping
How to Use Reflective Writing for Learning,
Teaching, Professional Insight and Positive Change
Dannelle D. Stevens and Joanne E. Cooper

"*Journal Keeping* is a superb tool for educators who want to be reflective practitioners, and help their students become reflective learners. But it is not a typical 'how-to' text, as the epigraph to Chapter 1 suggests: 'The unexamined life is not worth living.' Elaborating on Socrates, Stevens and Cooper explore the rationale, process and impact of journal keeping on educators and students alike, helping us overcome familiar obstacles; e.g., 'How can you possibly evaluate a student journal?' I hope this fine book will be widely read and used."— *Parker J. Palmer*, *author of* The Courage to Teach, Let Your Life Speak, *and* A Hidden Wholeness

"Dannelle Stevens and Joanne Cooper bring years of personal and professional experience with journal writing to inform the content of their book. This fact creates a level of credibility to their writing, and their approach to the material makes reading the text feel like a conversation with trusted friends. The intent of their volume is to explain the use of journaling in teaching and how to keep a journal to help organize professional lives. Therefore, this book should appeal to a variety of academic readers including faculty members, students, staff and administrators. In addition, both the novice and seasoned journal writer should find several takeaways . . . Among the several strengths of the book is the potential for immediate application of journal writing strategies to support active learning . . . *Journal Keeping* should be on everyone's short list. The writing is approachable, the book well organized and the material easy to implement in practice. Rarely have I found a book that I have been so enthusiastic about and that I highly recommend it to others."— *Community College Review*

22883 Quicksilver Drive
Sterling, VA 20166-2102

Subscribe to our e-mail alerts: www.Styluspub.com